Excel

ADVANCED SKILLS

ENGLISH

YEAR 5

AGES 10–11

SPELLING AND VOCABULARY WORKBOOK

Get the Results You Want!

Kristine Brown

Reprinted 2008, 2009, 2010, 2013, 2014, 2016, 2017, 2019, 2020, 2021, 2022, 2023

ISBN 978 1 74125 265 1

Pascal Press
PO Box 250
Glebe NSW 2037
(02) 9198 1748
www.pascalpress.com.au

Publisher: Vivienne Joannou
Series developer: Kristine Brown
Project editor: Mark Dixon
Edited by Mark Dixon
Reviewed by Carolyn Lain and Claire Balaam
Typeset by Grizzly Graphics (Leanne Richters)
Cover and page design by DiZign Pty Ltd
Printed by Vivar Printing/Green Giant Press

Acknowledgements
The publisher wishes to thank the people and organisations who gave their kind permission to reproduce copyright material. Specific acknowledgements appear under each text.

All efforts have been made to gain permission for the copyright material reproduced in this book, but we have not been successful in contacting all the copyright holders. The publisher welcomes any information that will enable rectification of any reference or credit in subsequent editions.

Contents

To the student

This book is about words: what they mean and how to spell them. It gives you **strategies** to learn new words and lots of **practice** in using these strategies. By the end of the book, you'll feel more confident attempting and learning new spellings and working out the meanings of new words.

Each unit is built around a theme or topic, for example *Life stories*, *Time to celebrate* and *In my opinion*. In each unit, you will find ten main sections.

Quick fun

This is a quick puzzle to introduce you to the unit theme. It should stretch your brain a little.

Topic spelling list

The **Topic spelling list** is a list of twenty words related to the unit theme. You might find some lists and words easier than others, but you should try to conquer them all. Take note of the **Spelling strategy** next to each list. It will help you with all the spelling you have to do throughout the unit.

Use the lines provided to write out the words using the **LOOK-SAY-COVER-WRITE-CHECK** method explained on the next page, and any other strategies that work well for you.

Fill in the gaps

The **Fill in the gaps** activity makes you think about the meanings of the words in the **Topic spelling list.** Only do this activity when you feel confident about the spellings. You will need to look back at the list to choose each word, but once you have chosen it, try to write it in the gap without looking back. This will test your brain a little more—which is good! In some units, you will also find a **Word scramble** to give you extra practice in spelling the topic words.

Killer words

The **Killer words** section contains five or six common words that students of your age often have trouble spelling. It also has some tips for remembering them and one quick activity. These words are not necessarily long, but they are all tricky. You should make a special effort to learn these words now and forever because you *will* need them! Use the memory tips given and the LOOK-SAY-COVER-WRITE-CHECK method.

One good idea for tricky words is to write them out in large letters and stick them on your bedroom wall or somewhere you will see them every day. Only take them down when you are absolutely sure that you know them.

Looking at ...

In this section, you will look at an important spelling pattern or rule. In some units, you will look at more than one. Again, it is important to learn the pattern and the words using the LOOK-SAY-COVER-WRITE-CHECK method and any other tricks you know. The activities in this section give you practice in writing the words and thinking about their meaning.

Proofreading

Proofreading gives you a chance to use your spelling knowledge to check someone else's spelling. Try to do it without looking back at the lists.

Vocabulary power

This section looks at different ways to expand your knowledge about words and meanings, and gives you practice in using new words and expressions.

Read and learn

The **Read and learn** section is very important because it gives you practice in expanding your vocabulary in the best way possible—through reading! You might find some of the questions difficult, but that's OK. This section is meant to challenge you.

Puzzle

Here you'll find a puzzle using the words from the unit. You'll find crosswords and wordsearches and sometimes quite 'cryptic' clues (*cryptic* means *hidden, not obvious*).

Your turn to write

Of course, we only need to learn spellings because we need to write. So here is your chance to use the words you have learnt in the unit in a real piece of writing. You'll also be able to use words you have learnt in the **Vocabulary power** section. You will need to use your own paper. Always revise and edit your writing for ideas, spelling, punctuation and grammar before writing out a final draft.

Other features

You'll also find some other features here and there: **Dictionary search**, **Do you know this word?** and **Did you know?** Take time to look closely at these. They will broaden your knowledge about the wonderful world of language.

Review units

There are four **Review** units. These will test your spelling of words in the previous five units. You should test yourself and then get someone else to test you—perhaps Mum or Dad.

I hope you enjoy working through the book. Good luck and have fun!

LOOK-SAY-COVER-WRITE-CHECK METHOD

The best way to learn new spellings is the **LOOK-SAY-COVER-WRITE-CHECK** method. You probably know this already, but here's a quick reminder.

- **LOOK** hard at the word.
  Think about the meaning. If you don't know the meaning, find it out.
  Think about patterns in the word. Does it follow the same pattern as other words you know?
  Underline the difficult letters that are especially hard to remember.
  Think about the look of the word. Take a picture of it mentally.
- **SAY** the word out loud, thinking about how it breaks up into syllables.
  Close your eyes and picture it in your mind while you say it. Write it in the air if you want to.
- **COVER** the word up and **WRITE** it without looking back.
- **CHECK** it. If you get it right, write it once more. If you get it wrong, do the **LOOK-SAY-COVER-WRITE-CHECK** method again until you get it right.

1 Life stories

Quick fun

How many words can you find in the word GRANDPARENTS in 60 seconds? Get someone to time you. There are at least 20, but you might find more. Write them in the box below.

Topic spelling list

born
lived
died
birth
death
grew up
years
youngest
eldest
adult

children
childhood
ancestors
originally
married
famous
parents
experiences
biography
adventures

Super strategy

Remember to use the **LOOK-SAY-COVER-WRITE-CHECK** method (page 1) to learn new words.

Try it out now on the words in the **Topic spelling list**. Write them in the line spaces on this page. Did the method work well for you?

Use this space to write out your topic words the first time. Use your own paper for extra practice.

Rewrite here those you had most trouble with.

Fill in the gaps

Fill in the gaps with words from the **Topic spelling list**.

1. The __________ artist, Leonardo da Vinci, was __________ in 1452 and died in 1519. He __________ in Italy during the period we call the Italian Renaissance.
2. Thomas Edison, the inventor of the electric light bulb, was one of seven __________.
3. Beethoven began studying piano and violin when he was four __________ old.
4. My mother is __________ from Malaysia, but all her __________ came from China.
5. My father __________ up in Italy, but his family moved to Australia when he was a teenager.
6. My __________ were married overseas. They had many interesting travel __________ before they settled down and had four children.
7. My mother is going to write a __________ of my great-grandmother, so that we will understand what a wonderful woman she was.
8. My eldest sister is getting __________ next year, but my mother thinks she is too young.
9. Do you think the __________ or the __________ child has the most fun?
10. The __________ of my great-grandfather was very sad because he missed the __________ of his twelfth grandchild two days later.
11. I don't understand why people sometimes say that __________ is the best time of your life. I can hardly wait to be an __________ and have lots of exciting __________.

Word scramble

Which words from the **Topic spelling list** are scrambled below?

1. RIRDEMA __________
2. SOMFAU __________
3. PRESCEENIEX __________
4. DENRILCH __________
5. LYALGINROI __________
6. RAPTENS __________
7. SURETENDAV __________
8. CANSROSTE __________

Killer words

Study the words and tips and then write them without looking back.

remember	Say it out loud. Listen to the syllables: *RE-MEM-BER*.	____________
remembering	Just add ***ing***.	____________
remembered	Just add ***ed*** (even though you don't hear it clearly).	____________
friends	Remember: *I see my FRI-ends on FRI-day*.	____________
people	A terrible word! Get the **pe** right (it is just as it sounds) and you won't mix up the **e** and **o**.	____________

Fill in the gaps with the five **Killer words**.

____________ don't always ____________ the names of those they meet. My mother even has trouble ____________ the names of her children and ____________! My great-grandmother is quite different. She has ____________ every one of her great-grandchildren's birthdays for the last twelve years and she has twenty to remember. Amazing!

Looking at … short e sound spelt *ea*

Most words with a short **e** sound are spelt with an **e**, e.g. ***e**ldest*, *m**e**t*, *b**e**d*, but many common words use **ea** to make this sound, e.g. *d**ea**th*, *h**ea**d*.

1. Look at the **ea** words below and take notice of the patterns, e.g. *d**ea**th*, *br**ea**th*. Then write the words in the spaces provided, grouping them in a way that will help you remember them. Look in your dictionary for the meanings of any words you do not know.

head	health	death	pleasant	feather	weapon	heaven
dead	weather	treasure	wealth	bread	spread	heavy
stealthy	measure	ready	pleasure	tread	peasant	jealousy
dread	leather	threat	steady	thread	breath	deaf

2 Use the clues to complete the ***ea*** puzzle below.

a		E	A					
b			E	A				
c		E	A					
d		E	A					
e			E	A				
f			E	A				
g			E	A				
h			E	A				
i		E	A					
j		E	A					

Clues

- **a** You'd rather be alive.
- **b** Another word for *fear.*
- **c** Two answers are possible: you might aim for both in your life.
- **d** Disliking someone who has got what you want.
- **e** Enjoyable.
- **f** If you find this, you'll have one of the possible answers for **c**.
- **g** In secret.
- **h** You need this to live.
- **i** Coming, ___________ or not!
- **j** You might become this in your old age!

Proofreading

Can you correct the spelling mistakes in this student's family story?

My great-granparents came to Australia from Greece in 1950. My great-granfather says he rembers the trip here by boat, and how sad he was to be leaving the small town where he was borne and grewup, and where his ansesters had livd and dide. He was the yungest of twelve childern, and so he was leaving behind many brothers and sisters as well as frends. My greatgranmother was sad to leave her perrents, but she was very happy to come to new country. They were not welthy peple and so when they arrived, life was very difficult. They often tell us about their experences and aventures when they first arrived and all the mistakes they made with English. We love to hear them talk about my grandfather's chilhood.

Vocabulary power

When two words have **similar meanings**, they are called **synonyms**. For example:

famous and *well-known*; *married* and *wed*.

Most synonyms have slight differences in meaning or are used in slightly different ways.

1 Draw lines to match the synonyms in the box below. They are all words you might use when writing about someone's life. Use your dictionary to look up any words you do not know.

brothers and sisters	children	teenager	content
ancestors	bring up	yearly	marriage
died	motherly	happy	origin
maternal	union	paternal	annual
siblings	goal	time	birthplace
forebears	raise	passed away	feat
ambition	offspring	memory	adolescent
achievement	fatherly	period	remembrance

2 Make up five **true** sentences about your family using some of the words above and words in the **Topic spelling list**. Ask your teacher or one of your parents to check your work.

Reminder
Check your punctuation.

Read and learn

Working out meanings of new words as you read is the best and easiest way to expand your vocabulary. Sometimes you might only guess a very general meaning, but often this is enough to understand the text.

Read this short text right through, and try to work out the meanings of the words in **bold**. Even if you have not read any of Roald Dahl's books, you should be able to work out most of the meanings.

Roald Dahl is surely one of the most successful and most beloved children's writers of all time. He upset many adult critics with his taste for cruelty and rudeness to adults, but children have always loved his unusual, sometimes **grotesque** sense of humour. His childhood experiences at boarding school later **inspired** him to write stories in which children fight against wicked and cruel adults.

Perhaps Dahl's most popular and well-known book is *Charlie and the Chocolate Factory*. In this wonderful story, one small, kind-hearted boy from an **impoverished** family bids for a prize in a competition with some highly unpleasant children who **come to sticky ends** because of their greediness. Most of Dahl's children's books dealt with this classic theme: **virtue** is rewarded and **vice** is punished.

1 Now circle the answer which best gives the meaning of each word or expression **a–f**. Before you choose your answer, reread the sentence in which each word occurs.

a	grotesque	**i**	unpleasant	**ii**	funny
b	inspired	**i**	gave him the ability to	**ii**	made him want to
c	impoverished	**i**	poor	**ii**	unhappy
d	come to sticky ends	**i**	end up in a bad way	**ii**	learn a lesson
e	virtue	**i**	sense of humour	**ii**	goodness
f	vice	**i**	badness	**ii**	rudeness

2 Look at the text again and underline any words you are unsure of. Look in the dictionary to find their meanings.

Do you know this word?
The verb ***reminisce*** means to talk or write about past experiences that you remember with pleasure, for example: *My grandfather likes to **reminisce** about his years working in outback Australia.*
The noun ***reminiscence*** is the act of remembering.

Puzzle

How many words from the unit can you find in this wordsearch? There are 30.
Words can be from the **Topic spelling list**, **Killer words** or **Looking at ...** sections.

B	E	E	U	Q	V	E	A	F	A	M	O	U	S	D	E	A	T	H	S	A	R	G	F	P	A	R	E	N	T	S	R
E	X	E	N	F	B	A	N	S	W	E	A	L	T	H	R	C	Y	A	T	U	Y	R	O	L	I	V	E	D	O	M	E
T	P	E	O	P	L	E	Q	O	P	N	S	E	Y	O	U	D	E	A	F	W	O	E	O	M	E	B	I	R	T	H	L
A	E	B	W	C	A	E	C	H	I	L	D	R	E	N	M	A	B	Q	S	E	U	W	M	A	E	B	W	C	A	Z	R
F	R	I	E	N	D	N	A	E	E	L	D	E	S	T	P	I	R	B	T	A	N	E	P	E	A	S	A	N	T	M	A
O	I	M	K	R	O	X	T	A	V	P	L	M	Y	E	A	R	S	E	M	P	G	F	E	R	S	S	N	N	I	R	L
H	E	A	L	T	H	T	H	V	O	Q	T	H	R	E	A	T	C	R	D	O	E	B	B	I	O	G	R	A	P	H	Y
E	N	O	V	A	B	S	Q	E	P	R	M	X	L	F	G	H	R	M	I	N	S	J	I	A	D	U	L	T	L	A	M
N	C	P	C	Y	O	E	O	N	A	A	D	V	E	N	T	U	R	E	E	U	T	G	M	R	E	M	E	M	B	E	R
M	E	O	N	O	R	V	X	R	Q	M	C	H	I	L	D	H	O	O	D	G	O	R	I	G	I	N	A	L	L	Y	D
R	S	A	N	U	N	H	M	A	R	R	I	E	D	G	O	L	I	O	B	A	N	C	E	S	T	O	R	S	N	N	Q

Your turn to write

Write a short biography of someone in your family, perhaps a grandparent or great-grandparent. You might need to get some information from this person or another member of your family. Here are some questions you could ask them, but you could also make up your own questions. Some questions might not be appropriate.

- When and where were you born?
- Where did you grow up?
- When did you come to Australia?
- How many children do you have?
- What interesting experiences and adventures have you had in your past?
- Where did your ancestors come from?
- What was it like in your childhood?
- When did you marry?

Do your writing on your own paper, but make sure you do a rough draft first. Revise and edit your work, and then write it out again.

☞ Answers on page 144

2 The working world

Quick fun

Can you fill in this no-clue crossword with words meaning work?

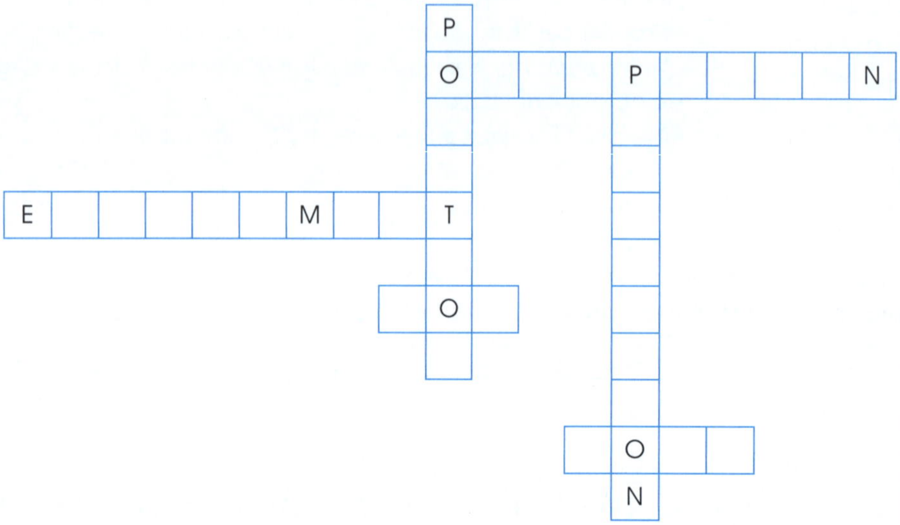

Use this space to write out your topic words the first time. Use your own paper for extra practice.

Topic spelling list

builder	doctor
designer	actor
manager	professor
photographer	assistant
soldier	musician
chemist	librarian
journalist	comedian
scientist	secretary
instructor	accountant
architect	mechanic

Top tip

When you're not sure of a word, write it out in two or three different ways. See which way looks right. Often you'll recognise the correct spelling when you see it:

~~cemist~~ ~~kemist~~ *chemist* √

Learn the words from the **Topic spelling list** now and write them out in the space provided using the LOOK-SAY-COVER-WRITE-CHECK method. Use the **Top tip** if you need to.

Rewrite here those you had most trouble with.

Fill in the gaps

Fill in the gaps with words from the **Topic spelling list**. You might need to change some words to plurals.

1. The ______________ asked the children to choose two books each.
2. Most film directors have two or three ______________ directors who help them.
3. Mum took the prescription the ______________ had given her to the local ______________.
4. My swimming ______________ used to be a national champion.
5. A ______________ reports the news.
6. An ______________ is someone who helps you with your finances.
7. The ______________ told us to say 'cheese', but it made us all look terrible.
8. Mum says I should be a ______________ or an ______________ because I like building things, but Dad says I should be an ______________ because I am always performing.
9. Nowadays there are not so many ______________ because everybody does their own typing and paperwork on computers.
10. Mum wants one of us to be a car ______________ so we can fix her car for free.
11. Don't ever think of becoming a ______________ with those corny old jokes.
12. ______________ are like teachers, except they work at universities and do research as well as teach.

Killer words

Study the words and tips and then write them without looking back.

busy	Remember that **bus** drivers are **bus**y people.	______________
business	Remember to change the ***y*** (bus**y**) to ***i***.	______________
were	Always think of ***we we***re to get this right.	______________
interest	Say the three syllables clearly: *IN-TER-EST*.	______________
worked	Remember: it's the past tense of *work*. Say *work-ED* to remind you of the silent **e**.	______________

Can you make up one sentence using ALL the **Killer words**? You can use *busily*, *interested* or *interesting* instead if you like. If you can't manage it in one sentence, use two.

____

____

____

____

____

____

Looking at ... *wh* words

Wh only occurs in front of a small number of words. Many of them are **question words**, e.g. ***wh**at*. Learn them now and you'll know them forever. **Wh** is usually pronounced ***h*** in front of **o**, e.g. ***wh**o*, ***wh**om* and ***wh**ole*.

what	who	whatever	wharf	whisker
when	whom	wherever	whip	white
where	whose	whenever	while	whimper
why	who's	whichever	whistle	wheel
which	whereas	whether	whisper	wheat

1 Which ***wh*** word am I thinking of?

a A word meaning *who is* ____________.

b A question word about a person ____________.

c A question word about place ____________.

d A word to ask the reason ____________.

e A question about ownership ____________.

f Speaking very softly ____________.

g Sounds the same as *witch* ____________.

h A question word rhyming with *lot* ____________.

i A question word about time ____________.

j To ____________ should I speak?

k ____________ the lambs went, Mary followed.

l A word that means the same as *if* ____________.

m A ***wh*** word used to compare ____________.

n a very important invention ____________.

Looking at ... apostrophe of possession

We use an **apostrophe** to show that a person or thing **owns or possesses** another. For example: *Joshua's father is a builder* (Joshua's father = the father of Joshua).

You only have to remember **one thing** about where to put the apostrophe. You put it **immediately after** the person/thing that does the owning. For example:

Joshua's father	= the father of <u>Joshua</u>	→ apostrophe goes after <u>Joshua</u>	→ Joshua's
the three builders' van	= the van of the three <u>builders</u>	→ apostrophe goes after <u>builders</u>	→ builders'
the children's uncle	= the uncle of the <u>children</u>	→ apostrophe goes after <u>children</u>	→ children's

1 Put apostrophes where needed in these sentences. For example:
The actors performance was brilliant, even though she had never acted before.
Answer: *The actor's performance was brilliant, even though she had never acted before.*

a I was allowed to stay in the mechanics workroom all day. It was great to watch them at work.
b The scientists prize was $50 000. He will use it for research.
c The accountants lunch took place yesterday. More than 100 people attended.
d The journalists stories were not published. Even worse, they lost their jobs.

2 Put an apostrophe if needed in these sentences. For example:
We met the actors after lunch. (No apostrophe is needed because the actors don't own anything.)

a The two professors agreed with each other.
b My doctors surgery is not far away.
c The young musicians van was broken into. He lost everything.
d The builders were late starting work.

Proofreading

Can you find the spelling mistakes? Some of the words might be from earlier units.

Wen I grow up I would like to have an intresting and bizzy job. My big brother used to say the same thing when he was little and now he werks as a landscape desiner. He travels all over the country, werever peple want him. I don't think I would want to werk outside all the time like him, but it would be good to find something witch always intersted me. At the moment, I'm thinking I might be a jurnalist because I like writing, although Mum says I will have to improve my spelling if I want to spend my life writing. My father thinks that I should be a sientist because that is wot he always wanted to be.

Vocabulary power

Knowing common **suffixes** (word endings) can sometimes help you make up words even if you have not heard them before. For example, you can sometimes work out what to call a job or occupation by trying out the common suffixes ***-er***, ***-or***, ***-ist***, ***-ant*** and ***-ian*** on base words.

The suffixes ***-er*** and ***-or*** are the most common endings and are usually added to verbs, e.g. *drive/driv**er**; sculpt/sculpt**or***.

The suffix ***-ist*** often means someone who does or studies something, e.g. *art/art**ist***. It is commonly added to words ending in ***-ology***, e.g. *ge**ology**/geolog**ist***.

The suffix ***-ian*** is often added to words ending in ***-ic***, e.g. *mus**ic**/music**ian*** or ***-y***, e.g. *librar**ian***.

1. Add the correct ending to the words in **bold** to make the occupation. You might have to change some letters, e.g. ***y*** to ***i***, or drop endings, e.g. **e** or ***al***.

   a Someone who **edits** books or films. ______________

   b Someone who studies **history**. ______________

   c Someone who studies **mathematics**. ______________

   d Someone who studies **optics** (eyes). ______________

   e Someone who works with **electric** systems. ______________

   f Someone who does **floral** arrangements or sells flowers. ______________

   g Someone who operates a **machine**. ______________

   h Someone who takes care of the **reception** desk. ______________

   i Someone who takes care of **technical** things. ______________

   j A doctor who treats a **special** area of the body. ______________

2. Draw lines to match the beginnings and endings of these occupations. The endings are in **bold**.

brick **programmer**   sold**yer**   hair**hand**   car**facturer**   kitchen**dresser**   pi**geant**   physio**lot**   den**tier**   computer **layer**   super**penter**   jack**ist**   manu**visor**   law**aroo**   ser**keeper**   sol**therapist**   book**icitor**

Dictionary search

An *-ologist* is one who studies or knows a lot about a certain subject. You probably know or can work out what these *-ologists* do: *biologist, zoologist, geologist, psychologist*.

However, you might not know these unusual *-ologist* occupations. Look up each one in the dictionary and jot down two or three words about what the *-ologist* studies. Use your own paper.

meteorologist	ornithologist	archaeologist	paleontologist
vulcanologist	oceanologist	anthropologist	futurologist
cryptologist	genealogist	seismologist	herpetologist

They all sound like interesting ways to spend your days, don't you think? Which one would you most like to be?

Did you know?

Many English surnames came from the jobs people used to do. For example, people with the name Baker originally got that surname from an ancestor who baked bread in a village or town.

Sometimes an occupation name was added to distinguish two people with the same first name. So if there were two 'Johns' in the village, the one who was a baker was called 'John the baker', and the one who was a farmer was called 'John the farmer'. Other occupation surnames are: Archer, Skinner, Draper, Gardener, Tailor and Cooper (maker of barrels).

Do you have a name derived from an occupation? Ask your parents if you are not sure. Even if a name does not seem to be an occupation name, it may be. For example, Baxter is also a word for a baker.

Read and learn

When we read, we often have to make guesses about word meanings based on familiar word parts. For example, we could probably work out that the past occupation *wheelwright* is a person who makes wheels.

Draw lines to match these past occupations to the kind of work they did. Each word has a part that will give you a clue.

turnkey	put up signs and advertisements
alchemist	cleaned houses for others
bill poster	turned ordinary metals into gold
fleshmonger	guarded prisoners
fowler	sold meat
ashman	farmed hens, ducks and other poultry
crier	helped drive cattle to market
charwoman	announced the important events in a town
cutler	took away the rubbish
ankle beater	sold and sharpened knives

Puzzle

Can you complete this crossword with words from the unit? The words might be from any section.

Across

2 Most people want work that is like this. (11)

3 ___________ pencil is this? (5)

4 You'll find a hat in this ***wh*** word. (4)

7 If you add an ***h*** to this word, you get a question about place. (4)

13 A ___________ might take still or moving pictures. (12)

14 This person plays tricks with our eyes. (8)

15 Unscramble this ***wh*** word: HREEWSA. (7)

16 I'm not sure ___________ to go or not. (7)

17 This person gets paid to pretend. (5)

18 The tooth fairy works with this person. (7)

Down

1 You'll find a bus in this office or company. (8)

3 The animal ___________ in pain. (9)

4 Take ___________ one you want. (9)

5 You have to practise, practise, practise if you want to be a ___________. (8)

6 Can you keep a secret? This person can. (9)

8 We often need this person when we are sick. (7)

9 What a joker! (8)

10 This person might work for a newspaper, radio station, TV station or website. (10)

11 You'll find this person at a university. (9)

12 She ___________ at the dog to make him return. (8)

Your turn to write

Write about the jobs some of your family members or friends do. Give their occupation and then describe the kinds of things they do in a day. You will probably need to ask them a few questions, so write these out first. Add some ideas about what kind of work you would or would not like to do when you grow up.

Do your writing on your own paper, but make sure you do a rough draft first. Revise and edit your work, and then write it out again.

Answers on page 145

3 Around the globe

Quick fun

Can you fill in the blanks to spell the important lines that mark the time and temperature zones on our globe? Use a globe or atlas if you need to.

1 E _ U _ T _ _

2 T _ O _ _ C _ _ C _ _ C _ _

3 T _ O _ _ C _ _
C _ P _ _ C _ _ _

4 _ N T _ _ C T _ C C _ R C _ _

5 A R _ _ _ _ C _ R C _ _

6 _ _ T _ _ N _ _ I _ N _ _
D _ _ E L _ N _

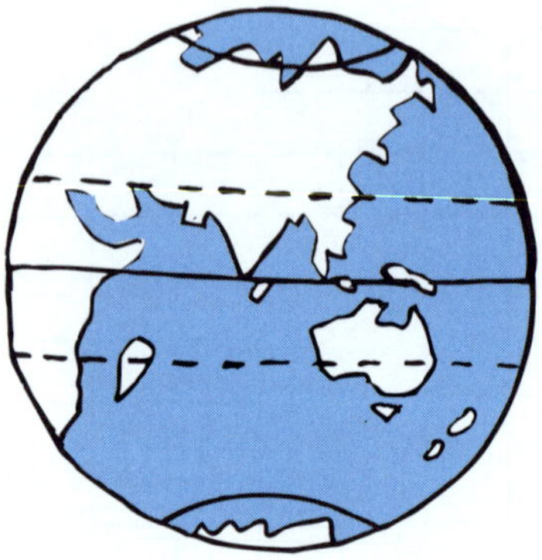

Use this space to write out your topic words the first time. Use your own paper for extra practice.

Rewrite here those you had most trouble with.

Topic spelling list

atlas	countries
zone	cities
continent	ocean
desert	circle
mountain	polar
tropics	region
horizon	area
island	temperature
longitude	atmosphere
latitude	hemisphere

Out-of-this-world advice

Writing out words in a way that reminds you of the difficult parts can help you remember them. For example: *atLAS, mountAIN,* etc.

Try this out with troublesome words from the **Topic spelling list**. Then write out all the words using the LOOK-SAY-COVER-WRITE-CHECK method.

Fill in the gaps

Fill in the gaps with words from the **Topic spelling list**. You might need to add an **s** to some words.

1. Twenty-six different ____________ have research stations on the Antarctic continent.
2. Hobart and Launceston are the two largest ____________ in Tasmania.
3. Australia is the only ____________ which is also an ____________.
4. ____________ and ____________ tell us exactly where a place is on the globe, even if it is in the middle of the ____________.
5. The ____________ are near the Equator. They have very high ____________ and lots of rain.
6. Most people don't realise that Antarctica is actually a ____________ because there are glaciers and ____________ in every direction.
7. My ____________ has many maps and interesting facts and figures about our planet.
8. Earth's ____________ is made up of six different layers of air and gases which protect life from the Sun.
9. Our planet is divided into two gigantic halves called ____________.
10. There are very few humans living within the Arctic ____________, but lots and lots of ____________ bears.
11. The world is divided into a number of climate ____________, for example: tropical, temperate and polar.
12. It is tempting to think that you could sail over the ____________, but of course you can't—it is always far, far away.

Killer words

Study the words and tips and then write them without looking back.

goes	Learn these two **oe** words together, even though the **o**	____________
does	sounds different. Remember the base words: *go*, *do*.	____________
doesn't	Remember: *doesn't* means *does not*.	____________
between	Don't forget the ***w***.	____________
because	Think of *because* and *cause* together and you'll be right.	____________

Can you make up one sentence using *all* the **Killer words**? If you can't manage it in one sentence, use two.

____

____

____

____

Looking at … plurals of words ending in *y*

When we make **plural nouns** from singular nouns ending in a ***consonant* + *y***, we change the ***y*** to ***i,*** and add ***es***. For example:

city → *cit**ies***   *count**ry*** → *count**ries***

We DON'T change the ***y*** to ***i*** if the noun ends in a **vowel** + ***y***. We just add **s**. For example:

*spra**y*** → *spra**ys***   *bo**y*** → *bo**ys***   *chimne**y*** → *chimne**ys***

Reminder
Nouns are naming words.

1. Make plurals from these singular nouns.

birthday ____________ decoy ____________ family ____________

spy ____________ body ____________ monkey ____________

jockey ____________ supply ____________ quay ____________

army ____________ quality ____________ lady ____________

party ____________ activity ____________ guy ____________

journey ____________ factory ____________ territory ____________

2. Can you unscramble these plurals? Some end in ***ies*** and some have a vowel + ***ys***.

a sbyuo ____________ (water markers)

b vocnyso ____________ (group of vehicles)

c eigsptis ____________ (found on a farm)

d yssrta ____________ (animals with no home)

e babyes ____________ (types of churches)

f bohbies ____________ (interests)

g lawlabsei ____________ (Australian animals)

h wbyusas ____________ (underground paths)

i bailtiise ____________ (skills)

3. Choose plurals from questions 1 and 2 above to use in these sentences.

a The adventurers transported their ____________ in three separate truck ____________.

b The two old ____________ had many ____________, but their favourite was taking care of animal ____________.

c The ____________ watched the men as they went about their daily ____________.

d ____________ must have superior mental and physical ____________.

Proofreading

Can you correct the spelling mistakes in this draft tourist brochure?

Brazil is the largest and most populous coutry in South America. You might be surprised to hear that in total arrea it is bigger than Australia and only slightly smaller than the United States. It covers a vast aria from above the Eqator in the north to below the Tropick of Cancer in the south. Brazil has varied terrain with low plains and hills in some regons, and mountins in others. The mighty Amazon River flows from east to west across the whole country. The temprature is mostly tropickal, particularly in the rainforests of the north. Brazil's capital city is Brasilia, but its largest and most well-known citys are Rio de Janeiro and Sao Paolo. It dosent matter where you travel in Brazil, becos werever you go, you will see sights that amaze and thrill you. What's more, you will meet the frendliest peple on Earth. Be prepared for the exspeariences and advenchers of a lifetime.

Vocabulary power

Prefixes are syllables which are added at the beginning of words, and which change the meaning of the base word. Prefixes are usually from the ancient Latin or Greek languages. If you learn the meanings of common prefixes, you will find it easier to understand new words.

1. The word *hemisphere* is from the Greek language. The prefix ***hemi-*** means *half*, so a *hemisphere* is *half a sphere*. However, the more common prefix for *half* is the Latin ***semi-***. For example: *semicircle*.

   Can you think of a ***semi*** word for these things?

   a A type of punctuation (half comma, half full stop). ____________________

   b A stage of competition just before the final. ____________________

   c A house which is joined to another house on one side. ____________________

   d A musical note. ____________________

   e Not completely conscious. ____________________

   f A type of big truck. ____________________

2. The words below begin with these Latin prefixes: ***circum-*** meaning *around*, ***co-*** meaning *with*, ***contra-*** meaning *against*. Can you work out the words?

   a CIRCUM _ _ R _ _ _ E — The distance around a circle.

   b CIRCUM _ _ AN _ _ S — The things going on around an event.

   c CO _ PE _ _ _ E — Work with someone on something.

   d CONTRA _ _ _ T — Say something opposite to what someone else says.

   e CIRCUM _ _ V _ _ _ _ E — Sail or move all the way around a place or thing.

   f CO _ D _ _ _ _ _ _ N — Education of both boys and girls together.

Read and learn

Remember: working out meanings of new words as you read is the best way to expand your vocabulary.

Read this short text right through, and try to work out the meanings of the words in **bold**.

Our world did not always look the way it does now. About 250 million years ago, there was just one massive super-continent called Pangaea. Fifty million years later, this super-continent had **fragmented** into two vast continents called Gondwanaland (including Australia) and Laurasia.

Today there are seven continents on Earth, and they are still moving at about two centimetres a year—about the same speed as your fingernail grows! Some scientists even predict that the continents will one day form one enormous super-continent once again as a result of constant **subterranean** forces. But don't worry—this won't happen for millions of years!

Do you know this word?

An *axis* (plural *axes*) is a real or imaginary straight line which goes through the centre of a spinning object. For example:

The Earth revolves around the axes which join the North and South Poles.

An axis is also a line which divides a symmetrical shape into two halves, or a line on a graph.

The **theory** of continental **drift** was first **proposed** by a German scientist called Alfred Wegener in 1912. Though his theory that the continents could (and did) move sparked only **scorn** and ridicule during his lifetime, his ideas are now widely accepted.

1 Now circle the answer which best gives the meaning of each word **a–f**. Before you choose your answer, re-read the sentence in which each word occurs.

a fragmented
- **i** broken up
- **ii** smashed

b subterranean
- **i** below the Earth
- **ii** oceanic

c theory
- **i** description
- **ii** idea to explain something

d drift
- **i** sudden movement
- **ii** slow movement

e proposed
- **i** asked scientists about
- **ii** put forward to other scientists

f scorn
- **i** lack of respect
- **ii** respect

2 Look at the text again, and underline any words you are unsure of. Look in the dictionary to find their meanings.

Did you know?

The word *atlas* comes from the name of a Greek demigod, Atlas, who was condemned forever to support the sky on his shoulders. The very first book of maps showed Atlas with the world on his back, and from then on, a book of maps has been called an *atlas*.

Puzzle

Can you do this cryptic word puzzle?

1. Take one letter from **atlas** and get a word to show regret. _ _ _ _
2. Change one letter of **zone** to get a past tense form of *do.* _ _ _ _
3. Find the metal in the middle of **continent**. _ _ _
4. Add a letter to the middle of **desert** to get something you might eat. _ _ _ _ _ _ _
5. Take the middle out of **mountain** to get a word meaning *most important*. _ _ _ _
6. Change the first syllable of **island** to something cold and get a country's name. _ _ _ _ _ _ _
7. Substitute two new letters for the first letter of **latitude** to get thanks. _ _ _ _ _ _ _ _ _
8. Find a maths word in **countries.** _ _ _ _ _
9. Think of a word that rhymes with **ocean** but has a completely different spelling. It means movement and begins with ***m***. _ _ _ _ _ _
10. Change the first letter of **polar** to get a kind of tooth. _ _ _ _ _
11. Change the first letter of **region** to get a group of soldiers. _ _ _ _ _ _
12. Think of a word for a facial mark from an injury. Add it to the front of **city** and get a word meaning *shortage*. _ _ _ _ _ _ _ _
13. Drop the last letter and add two more to make an adjective from **atmosphere.** _ _ _ _ _ _ _ _ _ _ _
14. Add a letter to the front of **horizon** and take one off the end to make a Spanish sausage. (Difficult! Ask your Mum or Dad.) _ _ _ _ _ _ _

Your turn to write

Imagine you are an explorer and that you have discovered a new land. Write a short letter back home telling people exactly where it is and what it is like. Use an atlas to help you. Use words from the list in your letter and lots of imagination!

Do your writing on your own paper, but make sure you do a rough draft first. Revise and edit your work, and then write it out again.

Answers on page 146

4 Time to celebrate

Quick fun

Can you unscramble this word? It spells the name of something used to celebrate special events. Another word for it is PYROTECHNICS. Use your dictionary if you're really stuck.

WKREIFOSR __ __ __ __ __ __ __ __ __

Use this space to write out your topic words the first time. Use your own paper for extra practice.

Topic spelling list

cheer
crowd
feast
festival
gala
display
annual
annually
celebrate
celebration
anniversary
holiday
tradition
parade
spectator
ceremony
procession
entertainment
commemorate
applause

Spectacular strategy

There is always **at least one letter for each sound** in a word. Sometimes there is more than one, but if you put at least one letter for each sound, you will avoid some spelling errors. For example:

entertainment ✓ *entainment* ×
annual ✓ *annul* ×

Learn and write out all the words from the **Topic spelling list**. Say difficult words out loud to make sure you put at least one letter per sound.

Word scramble

Which words from the **Topic spelling list** are scrambled below?

1. BRATELEEC ______________
2. SLAUEPAP ______________
3. EMMMROCOTEA ______________
4. DALHOIY ______________
5. NIOSESORPC ______________
6. YOCMREEN ______________
7. LUANAN ______________
8. ROTCATEPS ______________

Rewrite here those you had most trouble with.

Fill in the gaps

Use words from the **Topic spelling list** in these sentences. You might have to add an ***s*** or ***ed*** to some words.

1. My parents ____________ their fifteenth wedding ____________ last weekend.
2. The ____________ gathered to watch the ____________ pass by.
3. The ____________ included singing, dancing, brass bands, clowns and magic shows.
4. Our school fete is held ____________ in October.
5. The audience broke into enthusiastic ____________ when the show began.
6. The Anzac Day service ____________ all those who had fought in the war.
7. It is a ____________ in our family to decorate the house and garden each Christmas.
8. The best paintings went on ____________ in the community centre.
9. There were loud ____________ from our families when we marched by in the ____________.
10. Many countries have a ____________ to celebrate their most important cultural traditions.
11. When our family gathers for a ____________, we always have a gigantic ____________.
12. When we visited my family overseas, we loved going to the traditional ____________ in the little towns and villages.

Killer words

Study the words and tips and then write them without looking back.

special	Say: *It is spe**c**ial and ex**c**iting in the **c**ity* to	____________
exciting	remember the soft **c** in these words.	____________
especially	Remember the double ***l***.	____________
excitement	Break into *excite* and *ment*. Don't drop the **e**.	____________
surprise	Say: *You are (UR) a big surprise* to remember the ***ur***.	____________

Can you use all the **Killer words** in one sentence of less than 20 words?

____

____

____

____

Looking at … *tion* words

Many nouns are made by adding the suffix ***-tion*** (pronounced **shun**) to a word or word root. For example: *celebra**tion**, tradi**tion**, exhibi**tion***. We sometimes change the ending of the word before we do this, e.g. *celebrate* → *celebra**tion***, *describe* → *descrip**tion***.

1. Learn these ***tion*** words and then work out which words are jumbled up below.

station	nation	location	action	attraction
direction	demonstration	information	conversation	attention
competition	fiction	commotion	description	position

a CTDIREION ____________ b TANION ____________

c CITFION ____________ d TMOMOCION ____________

e TASTION ____________ f TALCOION ____________

g TARTATCION ____________ h AFORMNITION ____________

2. Now choose **five** words to use in your own sentences. Try to write sentences about festivals or celebrations, so that you can also use some words from the **Topic spelling list**.

____

____

____

____

____

3. Look at this fun graphic poem about ***tion*** words. Each picture is part of a story about a boy's haircut. Can you work out the story? Why is punctuation spelt *punktuation*?

____

____

____

Poem and drawing from *Mongrel Doggerel* by Elizabeth Honey, Allen & Unwin, 1998. Reproduced with permission.

Proofreading

Can you correct the spellings in this advertisement before it is put up around town?

> **SPESIAL event—come selebrate with us**
>
> Atracshens for yung and old: firewerks, bands and a Grand Perade
> All day entainment: **GLADSTONE GALAH DAY**
> To comemorate the day the railway came to Gladstone
> All spectors get free entry to train exibition
> Childern under five get a free balloon and train ride
> **Wen**? Saturday 12th July (second weekend of the school holydays)
> **Were**? Main Street, Gladstone
> Just follow the crouds!

Vocabulary power

Many words in the English language come from **Latin word roots**. For example, the word *com**memor**ate* has the Latin root ***memor*** meaning *memory*, and ***spect**ators* has the Latin root ***spect*** meaning *watch*.

If you take notice of similarities between words, you will gradually build up your knowledge of word roots. This will help you work out the meanings of new words.

1 Do you know these other ***mem*** words? Use your dictionary if you need to check spellings.

- **a** You must ___ ___ m e m ___ ___ ___ me. I met you last week.
- **b** My m e m ___ ___ ___ for faces is not very strong.
- **c** My aunty gave me a ring as a m e m ___ ___ ___ ___ of her visit.
- **d** My trip to Italy was m e m ___ ___ ___ ___ ___ ___.

2 Do you know these other ***spect*** words?

- **a** My Dad always uses the old-fashioned word s p e c t ___ ___ ___ ___ s for glasses.
- **b** The light show was absolutely s p e c t ___ ___ ___ ___ ___ ___.
- **c** I am coming there now to ___ ___ s p e c t your work.
- **d** The teacher has the ___ ___ s p e c t of the whole class.

3 Find three words in the **Topic spelling list** containing the letters ***ann***. Write the words below and then write what you think the Latin root ***ann*** means.

______________________ ______________________ ______________________

The word root ***ann*** means ______________________.

Dictionary search

Find one word beginning with ***mem*** which is about memory. Write down the meaning in your own words.

____

Find two other words beginning with ***spect***. Write down the meanings in your own words.

____

Read and learn

Read this extract from a tourist handbook and try to work out the meanings of the words in **bold**.

La Tomatina

Did you know that there is a festival where you are actually encouraged to throw tomatoes at other people? It's true. On the last Wednesday of every August, the small town of Bunol, in Spain, erupts into an enormous tomato fight! The battle takes place at the end of a week-long celebration, but even though there are fun festivities and events every day and night, the tomato battle is **undeniably** the festival highlight.

How did such a festival begin? Well, the story goes that during the forties, some friends started a tomato fight. It is still not quite clear why it started, but anyhow, before long, everyone was having a great time. They had so much fun that from that day on, the **fiesta** has been celebrated annually. It is now a major festival, called La Tomatina, which **coincides** with the festival of the town's patron saint.

For the week leading up to the **mammoth** battle, there are parades, musical bands, fireworks, food stalls and street parties. On the day, shopkeepers cover their windows and doors in preparation for the messy **onslaught**. Meanwhile, thousands of tourists and locals gather in the town square. Then, from the back of large trucks, a selected band of townsfolk start pelting the **throng** with ripe tomatoes. Then the crowds fight back, throwing the tomatoes (by now very squishy and messy) at anything and anyone. Soon the streets are **awash** with seeds, pulp and tomato skins.

It is usually all over in less than half an hour. Everyone then makes up with their fellow warriors and heads down to the river to clean up. Sounds like fun!

Do you know this word?

The adjective ***zany*** is used to describe something crazy, unusual and comical—like La Tomatina.

1. Now circle the answer which best gives the meaning of each word **a–g**. Before you choose your answer, re-read the sentence in which each word occurs.

a undeniably
- **i** definitely
- **ii** usually

b fiesta
- **i** festival
- **ii** meal

c coincides
- **i** takes place before
- **ii** takes place at the same time

d mammoth
- **i** exciting
- **ii** huge

e onslaught
- **i** attack
- **ii** event

f throng
- **i** queue of people
- **ii** crowd of people

g awash
- **i** covered in liquid
- **ii** cleaned up

2. Find the word *erupts* in the first paragraph. What do we usually talk of *erupting*? Why do you think the writer uses *erupts* here? ______________________________

____

3. Look at the text again and underline words you are unsure of. Look in the dictionary to find their meanings.

Did you know?

Have you heard of these unusual festivals?

- The Henley on Todd Regatta, a race in Alice Springs where people run in bottomless boats down a dry river bed. The event was only cancelled once—when rain was forecast.
- The Running of the Bulls in Pamplona, Spain, where crowds of people (mainly young men) let themselves be chased down the street by stampeding bulls.
- The Cheese Rolling of Cooper's Hill in Gloucester, England, where people roll themselves down a very steep hill after large wheels of cheese—with the aim of beating the cheese to the bottom.

Puzzle

Can you fill in the blanks with words from the unit (from any word list)?

1. Another word for *procession*. _ _ _ _ _ ☐
2. Do something to remember something or someone. ☐ _ _ _ _ _ _ _ _ _ _
3. A cultural custom. ☐ _ _ _ _ _ _ _ _
4. Time off school and work. _ _ ☐ _ _ _ _
5. Have a party or special event. _ _ _ _ ☐ _ _ _ _
6. Lots of people together. _ ☐ _ _ _
7. Happening every year. ☐ _ _ _ _ _ _ _
8. A cry of encouragement. _ _ ☐ _ _
9. An unexpected event, a shock. _ _ _ _ _ ☐ _ _
10. A match or contest. _ ☐ _ _ _ _ _ _ _ _ ☐

Now unscramble the letters in the boxes to make another word from the **Topic spelling list**.

______________________ → _ _ _ _ _ _ _ _ _ _

Your turn to write

Choose one of the following tasks. Do your writing on your own paper, but make sure you do a rough draft first. Revise and edit your work, and then write it out again.

1. Write an advertisement for a special event or celebration that occurs in your town or city. Make it attractive to the eye by using interesting lettering and pictures.

OR

2. Write about a traditional celebration in a culture you know about.

Answers on pages 146–147

5 In my opinion

Quick fun

What is your opinion on these questions?

1. What is your favourite way to spend your spare time?

____

2. Who is your role model? (Who influences your behaviour the most?)

____

3. What item would you most like to save for?

____

4. If you use the Internet, what do you mainly use it for?

____

5. If you could change one thing about yourself, what would it be?

____

Do you think you have the same opinion as most children? You can check on page 31 what the most common answers were in one Australia-wide survey.

Topic spelling list

viewpoint	reason
surely	believe
agree	perhaps
disagree	positive
argue	negative
argument	certainly
possible	totally
possibly	opinion
probable	really
probably	personally

Surefire strategy

It is always best to use a common spelling for a sound or syllable, unless you know different. For example, the long **e** sound is usually spelt **ee** *(agr**ee**)* and **ea** *(r**ea**son), while* **ie** *(bel**ie**ve)* is quite uncommon.

Write out and learn all the words from the **Topic spelling list**.

Use this space to write out your topic words the first time. Use your own paper for extra practice.

____

Rewrite here those you had most trouble with.

____

Fill in the gaps

Fill in the gaps with words from the **Topic spelling list**. You might have to make some words plural or add an ***ed***. There is sometimes more than one possible answer for each space.

1. We are doing a survey on homework. What is your ________________ on the subject?
2. My mother thinks that ________________ I should get more homework, but my father disagrees. He ________________ believes it's a waste of time.
3. We could ________________ about this question for weeks, but I will still ________________ with you.
4. ________________ you don't think he is right! I can't ________________ it.
5. My best friend ________________ disagrees with her parents about school uniform, so there is an ________________ every day.
6. My team was the affirmative in the debate. That means we ________________ with the statement. However, we lost to the ________________ team.
7. I did not think it was ________________ for us to lose. I'm so disappointed. Now we ________________ won't get into the final.
8. I can't ________________ agree with you. Your ________________ just don't make sense.
9. Yesterday Maria was absolutely ________________ about the matter, but today she might change her mind. ________________, I don't think she knows what she believes.

Killer words

Study the words and tips and then write them without looking back.

again	Learn *ag**ai**n* and *ag**ai**nst* together. Say *agAIn* and	________________
against	*agAInst* to spell them, not *agen* and *agenst*.	________________
thought	A very hard one! Spell it out loud till you know it.	________________
should	Learn *could*, *should* and *would* together. Then	________________
would	you'll have one problem, not three!	________________
could		________________

Use the **Killer words** to fill the gaps so that the paragraph makes sense.

If I ________________ I ________________ do it, I ________________, but I really think you ________________ do it yourself. I know you are ________________ the whole idea, but I tell you ________________ that everyone will support you, if only you try.

Looking at …words ending in *ly*

We often make adverbs by adding ***ly*** to adjectives. Usually we just add the ***ly***, e.g. *total* + ***ly*** → *total**ly***.

It is more difficult when the adjective ends in **e**. Sometimes we keep the **e**, e.g. *sur**e*** + ***ly*** → *sur**ely***. Sometimes we drop the **e**, e.g. *possibl**e*** + ***ly*** → *possib**ly***, *simpl**e*** + ***ly*** → *simp**ly***. Most ***able*** and ***ible*** words drop the **e**.

> **Reminder**
>
> **Adjectives** are words that describe a noun. For example:
> *I am in **total** agreement with him.*
>
> **Adverbs** are words that add information to verbs and adjectives. For example:
> *I **totally** agree with him.*

1 Match an ***ly*** word from the box to one in the list below which has a similar meaning.

definitely	particularly	sincerely	terribly	normally
initially	generally	actually	frankly	completely

a firstly ____________ b certainly ____________

c usually ____________ d really ____________

e especially ____________ f truly ____________

g honestly ____________ h awfully ____________

i mostly ____________ j wholly ____________

2 Use some of the ***ly*** words above to make **true** sentences about your opinions on these subjects. Tell us what you **really** think.

a wearing school uniforms ____________

____

b homework ____________

____

c compulsory sport in school ____________

____

d reality television ____________

____

Looking at … proverbs

Proverbs are short, well-known sentences that people use to express a common human experience or to give advice. *Love is blind*, for example, means that people in love often don't see the faults of the person they are in love with.

1 Can you fill in the missing words of these well-known proverbs? Even if you have not heard of them before, you can probably work them out.

words	perfect	heads	cake
beggars	blood	wise	pudding
hand	link	book	cat

- **a** Two ________________ are better than one.
- **b** Early to bed and early to rise makes you healthy, wealthy and ________________.
- **c** ________________ is thicker than water.
- **d** Actions speak louder than ________________.
- **e** Practice makes ________________.
- **f** A bird in the ________________ is worth two in the bush.
- **g** A chain is no stronger than its weakest ________________.
- **h** You can't judge a ________________ by its cover.
- **i** There is more than one way to skin a ________________.
- **j** The proof of the ________________ is in the eating.
- **k** ________________ can't be choosers.
- **l** You can't have your ________________ and eat it too.

2 Which proverb above would you use to encourage:

- **a** someone in a team to do their part? ____ *(write the letter)*
- **b** someone to stop talking and do something? ____
- **c** someone to put up with what they are given? ____
- **d** someone to help you with a problem? ____

Proofreading

Can you check the spelling of this letter to the editor before it is sent?

Dear Editer

I am writing to give my opinnion about the plan to build more houses in the bushland behind Murray Road. I can give you three resons why you shuld not do this. Ferstly, I don't want to see all those kangaroos, wallabys, frogs and birds being killed just for houses. Surly they can buld them somewere else. Personly, I think the animals have the right to the land—they were there first. Secondly, I reelly think that it will make the traffic worse on that road. I can't beleve you have not thort about this—so why woud you do it? Thirdly, I totaly agree with Koby Bruin who wrote to your paper last week. He gave a very good agument for not building: the residents in the new houses will be in danger from bushfires.

Vocabulary power

One excellent way to improve your word power is to use a **thesaurus**. A thesaurus is a book which groups together **words of similar meanings**.

For example: if you look up *opinion* in the *Macquarie Junior Thesaurus*, you will find these words listed: *attitude*, *outlook*, *viewpoint*, *stand* and *conviction*. It also gives the precise meaning of each word and an example of how it is used.

If you have the *Macquarie Junior Thesaurus*, use it now to find the page for *opinion* and read the five word entries. If you have another thesaurus, look in it for *opinion*. Are the entries the same as those given in the Macquarie?

Write down any other words here: ______________________________

Now use your thesaurus to look up these words. Write down three synonyms you find:

agree ______________________________

argument ______________________________

disagree ______________________________

Choose one from each group to write in sentences. You could write on the topics in the **Looking at …** section.

____

____

____

Read and learn

Always use your **own experience** to work out meanings of words you meet when reading.

Use your experience of the Internet to work out the meanings of the words in **bold** below.

Do you know this word?

A ***dilemma*** (noun) is a situation in which a difficult choice must be made between two possibilities. For example:

I'm in a ***dilemma****. Should I go horse-riding with my cousins or go to my best friend's birthday sleepover?*

What do you think of the Internet?

- It can be difficult to **sift through** the garbage.
- My mother was **keen** at first, but now she doesn't use it much at all. She prefers reading books.
- I don't believe it will **dominate** our lives. Nobody wants to spend all of their time in front of a computer.
- It's **not all it's cracked up to be**. I mean, is anyone smarter because of it?
- It definitely **facilitates** communication, especially from one side of the world to the other.
- The amount of information can be **overwhelming**.
- I'm still **skeptical** about the advantages of the internet. Basically I think it just wastes a lot of time.
- It has the **potential** to make the world a better place.

Choose one of the words in the box to use in place of each of those in **a**–**h** below.

doubtful	too much	power	makes easier
take over	separate	enthusiastic	not as good as people say

a sift through ______________ **b** keen ______________

c dominate ______________ **d** not all it's cracked up to be ______________

e facilitates ______________ **f** overwhelming ______________

g skeptical ______________ **h** potential ______________

Puzzle

How many words from this unit can you find in the wordsearch? There are 20 altogether.

R	Y	P	O	S	S	I	B	L	Y	X	I	P	N	U	K
F	P	N	P	E	R	H	A	P	S	H	O	R	O	H	Y
B	O	E	V	H	S	U	R	E	L	Y	P	O	T	R	I
C	S	G	I	Y	J	G	K	D	A	A	I	B	Q	B	S
E	I	A	E	R	Y	Z	Z	R	R	D	N	A	F	R	H
L	T	T	W	P	E	H	G	G	C	I	I	B	K	E	O
Y	I	I	P	W	M	U	U	K	Q	S	O	L	T	A	U
C	V	V	O	R	M	P	S	W	T	A	N	Y	A	L	L
E	E	E	I	E	E	O	H	O	U	G	S	I	R	L	D
R	T	U	N	N	Y	S	W	U	N	R	M	R	G	Y	A
T	H	T	T	P	J	S	P	L	S	E	I	E	U	Y	Q
A	O	M	K	Y	K	I	I	D	G	E	R	A	M	W	P
I	U	J	F	I	W	B	K	X	N	J	X	S	E	J	X
N	G	M	E	J	E	L	A	R	G	U	E	O	N	I	S
L	H	E	E	X	J	E	K	G	R	S	O	N	T	P	F
Y	T	O	T	A	L	L	Y	B	A	G	A	I	N	S	T

Your turn to write

Write a letter to the editor on a topic mentioned in this unit, such as the Internet, homework, or one of the topics in **Quick fun**.

- Say what you are writing about.
- Say what your overall opinion is.
- Give your reasons for your opinion.

Do your writing on your own paper, but make sure you do a rough draft first. Revise and edit your work, and then write it out again.

Quick fun answers

Responses to **survey questions** were:

- Favourite way to spend spare time: play ball sports 25%; spend time with friends 17%; outdoor activity 13%.
- Role model: parents 43%; other relatives 27%; sports stars 20%.
- Item to save for: computer/computer games 17%; sports equipment 14%; TV, stereo, CDs 12%.
- Internet use: schoolwork 72%; email 22%; chatting 14%; browsing 8%; downloading music 8%; games 8%; other 10%.
- Change something about yourself: almost 50% said they would like to be fitter, do better at school and be richer.

☞ Answers on page 147

Review 1

Now let's see what you remember of the words you learnt in Units 1–5. There are four tests in this review. You could do all in one session, or you could break them up and do them over a few days.

Step 1 Look at each group of words in the test to revise the spellings.

Step 2 Cover the five words up and test yourself (column 2). Try to do all five words in one go.

Step 3 Write your score out of 5 in the box. If you got any words wrong, go back and study them again.

Step 4 If possible, ask someone to test you on the words later—an hour or even a day later (column 3).

Test 1

Study	Test yourself	Test with another person
born lived died birth years	/5	/5
youngest eldest adult children ancestors	/5	/5
married famous parents experiences adventures	/5	/5
remembered friend people health soldier	/5	/5
head heavy builder designer manager	/5	/5
death scientist instructor journalist librarian	/5	/5
	Total score = out of 30	Total score = out of 30

Test 2

Study	Test yourself	Test with another person
musician actor accountant mechanic architect	/5	/5
whistle interest worked busy wharf	/5	/5
business wherever whenever whichever secretary	/5	/5
whereas while atlas continent desert	/5	/5
mountain horizon island latitude countries	/5	/5
cities ocean region area temperature	/5	/5
	Total score = out of 30	Total score = out of 30

Test 3

Study	Test yourself	Test with another person
atmosphere goes does families between	/5	/5
because birthdays doesn't bodies festival	/5	/5
activities guys journeys cheer crowd	/5	/5
gala annually parties celebration ceremony	/5	/5
anniversary holiday tradition spectators display	/5	/5
procession entertainment commemorate applause special	/5	/5
	Total score = out of 30	Total score = out of 30

Test 4

Study	Test yourself	Test with another person
exciting especially surprise location direction	/5	/5
demonstration information viewpoint surely disagree	/5	/5
argue argument possibly probably reason	/5	/5
believe perhaps positive certainly totally	/5	/5
opinion really personally actually against	/5	/5
thought should definitely particularly again	/5	/5
	Total score = out of 30	Total score = out of 30

Which word?

1. I don't know ______________ to go or not. (*weather*, *whether*)
2. Do you know ______________ going to the party? (*who's*, *whose*)
3. I don't know ______________ I'm going. (*were*, *where*)
4. Tell me ______________ one you want. (*witch*, *which*)

Well done. That's a lot of words you know how to spell!

☞ Answers on page 147

6 Life through the ages

Quick fun

Can you unscramble these civilisations from past times?

1. KIVGSNI _ _ _ _ _ _ _
2. ZTCEAS _ _ _ _ _ _
3. MAROSN _ _ _ _ _ _
4. YPTEIAGNS _ _ _ _ _ _ _ _ _
5. KGEERS _ _ _ _ _ _

Use this space to write out your topic words the first time. Use your own paper for extra practice.

Topic spelling list

battle
peaceful
kingdom
reign
ancient
period
war
warrior
soldier
pioneer

empire
emperor
conquer
invade
history
rebellion
colony
settlement
settler
century

Terrific tactic

Spelling words out loud can really help you remember them. This is because you are picturing the spellings in your head as you spell them.

It is also good to chant the spellings as if you are singing a song.

Spell all the words from the **Topic spelling list** out loud and then write them out.

Rewrite here those you had most trouble with.

Fill in the gaps

Fill in the gaps with words from the list. You might have to make some words plural or add an ***ed***.

1. Britain established many ____________ around the world, including Australia and New Zealand.
2. The 18th ____________ was a period of great exploration and discovery.
3. The first white ____________ in Australia lived in the area around Sydney Cove.
4. The Vikings were a race of fierce ____________, who ____________ the coastal areas of England and other countries around thirteen to fourteen hundred years ago.
5. There were many terrible ____________ fought in the First World ____________.
6. Queen Elizabeth has ____________ for more than 50 years.
7. The leaders of the ____________ were put in jail, but eventually the government met their demands.
8. Writing was invented 5 000 years ago by an ____________ civilisation called the Sumerians, who lived in the area now known as Iraq.
9. The ____________ before writing was invented is called *pre-history*, and the people who lived in these times are called *pre-historic*.
10. In ancient times, every country lived in fear of being ____________ by invading armies from nearby territories. ____________ times were very unusual.
11. One of the most well-known Roman ____________ was Nero, who is said to have played the fiddle while Rome burned.

Killer words

Study the words and tips and then write them without looking back.

known	You might hear *know-en*, but it is spelt *known*.	____________
discovered	Don't forget the **e** in the ***ed*** ending.	____________
through	Chant *through* and *during* out loud until you	____________
during	know them well.	____________
government	Use a spelling pronunciation: *GO-verN-ment*.	____________

Which of the **Killer words** contains the following words?

1. A kind of jewellery. ____________
2. The opposite of *smooth*. ____________
3. A colour. ____________
4. A word meaning *this minute*. ____________
5. A word meaning *above*. ____________ *(two possible answers)*

Looking at … *or* sound spelt *a* and *ar*

The **or** sound is usually written **or** or **ore**, e.g. *hist**or**y*, *st**ore***. However, it is also sometimes written with an **aw** (e.g. *dr**aw**, br**aw**l*), **au** (e.g. *c**au**se, p**au**se*), **ar** (e.g. *w**ar**, w**ar**m*) or **a** (e.g. ***a**lso, h**a**ll*). It is a good idea to look for patterns for tricky sounds like this. It will help you guess the spellings of new words.

1 Look for the patterns in the list of words below. Then complete these sentences:

The **or** sound is usually spelt _________ when following a ***w***, ***sw*** or ***kwa*** (spelt ***qu***) sound.

The **or** sound is usually spelt _________ in front of a double ***l*** or an ***l*** + consonant.

war	warm	ward	warden	all	bald	almost
warn	swarm	award	wardrobe	small	scald	always
wart	dwarf	reward	quarter	wall	chalk	baulk
warp	wharf	towards	swarthy	salt	talk	falter

2 Can you find a synonym from the list above for these words? Use your dictionary if you need to.

a	jetty	___________	b	battle	___________	c	speak	___________
d	guard	___________	e	cupboard	___________	f	burn	___________
g	advise	___________	h	prize	___________	i	hesitate	___________
j	nearly	___________	k	everyone	___________	l	hot	___________
m	dark-skinned	___________	n	midget	___________	o	gather	___________
p	change shape	___________	q	hospital room	___________	r	stop	___________

Looking at … regular past tenses

The usual way to make a **past tense verb** is to add ***ed***. Sometimes this is easy to hear and spell, e.g. *reward**ed**, defeat**ed***. Sometimes we don't hear an ***ed***, so it is easy to make mistakes with spellings. For example:

we say a ***t*** sound, e.g. *hop**ed**, lik**ed**, miss**ed**, wish**ed**, laugh**ed***

we say a ***d*** sound, e.g. *plann**ed**, flow**ed**, decay**ed**, pray**ed***

we say an ***ed*** sound, e.g. *need**ed**, want**ed***.

Reminder
Verbs are doing words.

1 Read these past tense verbs out loud. Next to each, write if the ***ed*** is pronounced ***ed***, ***t***, or ***d***. Learn any you are not sure of using the LOOK-SAY-COVER-WRITE-CHECK method.

invaded	_________	settled	_________	conquered	_________	battled	_________
reached	_________	crossed	_________	saved	_________	reigned	_________
hurried	_________	flashed	_________	attacked	_________	married	_________
lasted	_________	explored	_________	governed	_________	changed	_________
assisted	_________	liked	_________	hated	_________	camped	_________

Note: some irregular verbs end in ***t*** instead of ***ed***, e.g. *slep**t**, buil**t***. We'll look at these in Unit 17.

2 Use **five** of the verbs above with words from the **Topic spelling list** in short sentences. Use your own paper.

3 Remember that verbs ending in **e** usually drop the **e** before adding ***ed*** or ***ing***,
e.g. *hat**e*** → *hat**ed*** → *hat**ing***; *chang**e*** → *chang**ed*** → *chang**ing***.

Write the ***ed*** and ***ing*** forms of the verbs shown in the pictures.

a d ________ ________

b r ________ ________

c s ________ ________

d w ________ ________

e d ________ ________

f c ________ ________

g a ________ ________

h l ________ ________

Puzzle

See how you go with this cryptic word puzzle.

1. Take the ***y*** from **history** and add three letters to get a person who studies it. _ _ _ _ _ _ _ _ _
2. Change one letter of **battle** to get a sound. _ _ _ _ _ _
3. Find something that tinkles inside **rebellion**. _ _ _ _
4. Change one letter of **empire** to get a person who makes tough decisions. _ _ _ _ _ _
5. Add a letter to **reign** to get a word meaning to give up work. _ _ _ _ _ _
6. Add a letter to **war** to get a word meaning change shape (this happens to wood). _ _ _ _
7. Find some money spread out in **ancient**. _ _ _ _
8. Take the first two syllables from **pioneer** and add an ***s*** to get an unpleasant expression. _ _ _ _ _
9. Take the first syllable from **conquer** and add a ***y*** to get a question. _ _ _ _
10. Take the ***y*** from **century** and add three letters to get a Roman soldier. _ _ _ _ _ _ _ _ _

Proofreading

Can you check the spelling in this assignment about ancient Rome?

From the seventh to the fifth centruy BC, Rome was ruled by kings. Then the Romans set up a republic and elected their leaders. This workt well for many yeers until a powerful general called Julius Caesar took control in 45 BC. He was murderd five yeres later, and his nephew Octavian took over. Octavian changd his name to Augustus and became the first Roman empror.

The Roman army was very tough and well-trained, with experience in many wors and battels. After they conquerd all of Italy, Roman solders marched into other countrys and defeated their armys. The land they ruled over was called the Roman Empyre.

Do you know this word?

The noun ***monarch*** means a king or queen. A ***monarchy*** is a country ruled by a monarch. A ***monarchist*** is a person who supports a system of having a king or queen.

Durng this period, the Romans built many fine roads, bridges, towns and citys. The towns were planned to look like Rome, with a town centre, or forum, containing magnificent govement buildings and grand temples.

Eventually, the empyre ran into trouble. There were riots and rebelions and attacks from tribes called barbarians. Five hundred years after Augustus's rein, the city of Rome was burnt and allmost all the Empire destroyed.

Vocabulary power

Develop your word power by taking notice of **word families**. For example:
settle (verb): *They* ***settled*** *in Melbourne.*
settler (noun): *The* ***settler*** *was courageous.*
settlement (noun): *The* ***settlement*** *was a dangerous place.*

Fill in the chart with words from the same word family.

Note: Some words don't change their form from noun to verb, e.g. *battle* is both noun and verb. Also, some adjectives (describing words) are made by adding the suffix ***-ing***.

Noun	Verb	Adjective
colony		
	conquer	
	invade	
rebellion		
	explore	
	invent	
	develop	
	reign	

Read and learn

When doing a school project, you often have to read information written for older people. This usually means you meet new words. Always try to work out general meanings of the difficult words as you read, and then check the exact meanings later in your dictionary.

Read this information about the famous city of Pompeii.

Pompeii

Most evidence of human life in ancient settlements disappears long before archaeologists begin excavating. It either **disintegrates** or is lost over the centuries. Only rarely do they find a site preserved very much as it was in **antiquity**. This happened with the city of Pompei.

On the morning of 24th August AD 79 Mount Vesuvius, a volcano on the southern tip of Italy, erupted, burying the surrounding area under tonnes of volcanic ash and lava. The eruption sealed and preserved Pompei and the nearby town of Herculaneum.

When excavations took place in the 18th century, they provided **abundant** information about the lives of ordinary people who lived two thousand years ago. They even told us what people were doing at the time. This was because the ash which buried the people had hardened around them, providing **casts** of their body shapes which were then able to be filled with plaster to make life-like sculptures.

However, before this happened, the ruins were badly **plundered** for treasures to **adorn** royal palaces and the houses of the rich. Eventually an archaeologist called Guiseppe Fiorelli took control. He kept accurate records of the various finds and invented the method of plaster casts.

Now four-fifths of Pompei has been uncovered and restored, and visitors to the area can see shops, bars, laundries, gardens, theatres, restaurants, bathhouses, homes, furniture, pots, pans, kettles, scales and artworks. It is the most complete picture of life two thousand years ago that we have.

Now read it again, and make a guess at the meanings of the words in **bold,** and write your guesses below Then use your dictionary to check how close you were, and write the exact meanings in note form.

Word	Your guess at meaning	Meaning from dictionary
disintegrates		
antiquity		
abundant		
casts		
plundered		
adorn		

Your turn to write

Do you like watching television programs or films about historical events? About kings and queens? Wars and battles? Exploration and discovery? Or about everyday life?

Write about what you like and why, and give some examples. If you don't like historical programs, say why not.

Using your own paper, make sure you do a rough draft first. Revise and edit your work, and then write it out again.

7 Once upon a time

Quick fun

What a mess! Can you unscramble the titles of these well-known children's stories?

The Beauty's Clothes Muddle

____

Emperor and the Wombat

____

Little New Blinky Hood

____

The Red-Headed Kangaroo

____

The Adventures of Bill and the Beast

____

The Adventures of Riding Dot

____

Topic spelling list

heroine	villain
hero	castle
heroes	cruel
handsome	knight
prince	dragon
princess	dungeon
wicked	tower
wizard	ogre
witch	giant
rescue	courageous

Towering trick

A good trick for difficult words is to invent a **spelling pronunciation** for them. When learning them, say the words exactly as they are spelled.

For example: say *casT-le* (pronouncing the ***t***), *K- night* (pronouncing the ***k***), and *gi-ANT*.

Think of other spelling pronunciations for difficult words from the **Topic spelling list**. Then write the words using any strategies which help you.

Use this space to write out your topic words the first time. Use your own paper for extra practice.

____

Rewrite here those you had most trouble with.

____

Fill in the gaps

Fill in the gaps with words from the **Topic spelling list**. You might need to make some words plural.

1. An ________________ is a monster, usually a hideous giant who stays alive by eating human beings.
2. In many traditional fairy stories, there is a ________________, ________________ young man who turns out to be a sweet, kind and rich ________________.
3. In *Jack and the Beanstalk*, Jack climbs a beanstalk and meets a huge, horrid ________________ who lives above the clouds.
4. The characters in fairytales usually live happily ever after, and go off to live in magnificent ________________.
5. ________________ usually ride on white horses, fight ________________ and ________________ damsels in distress.
6. In traditional tales, the ________________ are usually very shy, quiet and beautiful.
7. In some modern fairytale versions, such as Walt Disney's *Beauty and the Beast*, the heroines are strong, brave and clever, and take part in as much action as the ________________.
8. Prisoners are usually kept in a dark ________________ underneath a castle, or at the top of a tall ________________.
9. In many tales, there is a very ________________, very ________________, very old ________________.
10. The Harry Potter stories have many classic elements of traditional fairytales: good, clever ________________, and cruel and nasty ________________.

Killer words

Study the words and tips and then write them without looking back.

character	Use a spelling pronunciation: say ***ch*** instead of a ***k*** sound.	________________
favourite	Both *favourite* and *favorite* are acceptable spellings.	________________
once	Remember ***one*** when spelling ***on**c**e***.	________________
happily	Remember to change the ***y*** in *happ**y*** to ***i*** in *happ**i**ly*.	________________
beauty	Say it like this: *be-A-uty.*	________________
beautiful	Remember to change the ***y*** to ***i*** in *beaut**i**ful*.	________________

Make up a very short story (one or two sentences only) using *once*, *happily*, *beauty* and *beautiful*.

____

____

Looking at … homophones

Homophones are words that sound the same. ***Homo*** means *same* and ***phone*** means *sound*. For example: *witch* and *which*; *knight* and *night*.

***Which** book did you like best? I liked the one about the wicked **witch**.*

*Last **night** I had a strange dream. I was being rescued from a dungeon by a handsome **knight**.*

1 Draw lines to match the homophone to its meaning. Use your dictionary if you're not sure.

a	weather	if	b	quite	silent	c	tale	story
	whether	climate		quiet	a little		tail	part of an animal
d	lesson	study time	e	aloud	permitted	f	piece	quietness
	lessen	reduce		allowed	with sound		peace	bit
g	through	tossed	h	dye	colour	i	strait	direct
	threw	between		die	pass away		straight	a narrow stretch of water
j	weak	seven days	k	except	but for	l	guest	predicted
	week	not strong		accept	take		guessed	visitor
m	there	belonging to them	n	to	a number	o	your	you are
	they're	they are		too	also		you're	belonging to you
	their	a place		two	opposite of *from*			

2 Choose the right word for each sentence.

a ____________ over ____________ in ____________ car. (*their, they're, there*)

b You're ____________ close ____________ the fire. Take ____________ steps back. (*to, too, two*)

c The princess said: 'I ____________ all the gifts ____________ for the one from my wicked stepmother.' (*except, accept*)

d ____________ supposed to be at ____________ music lesson by now. (*you're, your*)

e The princess ____________ the ring ____________ the hole in the curtain. (*through, threw*)

Looking at … changing *y* to *i*

If a word ends in **consonant + *y***, we change the ***y*** to ***i*** before adding any endings **unless** the ending starts with ***i***. For example: *marry* → *marriage* → *married* BUT *marrying*.

Add the endings given to the words below.

a	happy (er)	____________	b	easy (ly)	____________	c	heavy (ness)	____________
d	carry (age)	____________	e	pretty (er)	____________	f	carry (ing)	____________
g	pretty (ness)	____________	h	pray (ing)	____________	i	merry (ment)	____________
j	spooky (ly)	____________	k	pray (er)	____________	l	hungry (ly)	____________
m	empty (ness)	____________	n	clumsy (er)	____________	o	empty (ing)	____________

Proofreading

Can you check the spelling in this story summary?

My favrite farytail is *Cinderella*. *Cinderella* has all the classic caracters: the heartless, wikked stepmother, the ugly stepsisters, the hansome prinse and the pore bueatiful yung girl. It even has a fary godmother. Wen the King's son gives a ball, Cinderella is not aloud too go because of all the werk she must do. However, after her silly, spiteful sisters go off, Cinderella is rescude by her godmother who waves her majic wand, converting a pumpkin to a coach, six mice into horses and six lizards into footmen. She transforms Cinderella's ragged clothes and shoes into a beautyful dress and dainty glass slippers, and then sends her off—but with a warning to return by midnight. Of course, the prince falls in love with her strait away, but when the clock chimes twelve, Cinderella dashes off into the night. Luckily one of her slippers falls off in her haste to get away, and this enables the prince to find her the next day. To her foolish stepsisters' dismay, she and the prince mary and of course live hapyly ever after.

Vocabulary power

In traditional **fairytales**, certain words **go together** more than others. For example, we usually read about the *handsome prince* rather than the *nice-looking* or *attractive prince*.

1 Match the adjectives in the box with the nouns to make common story word pairs. Write them in the spaces.

magic	beautiful	wicked	enchanted	wicked	cruel
brave	ugly	rich	faithful	poor	royal
fire-breathing	gentle	magic			

a ____________ looking glass	**b** ____________ princess	**c** ____________ stepmother
d ____________ forest	**e** ____________ witch	**f** ____________ queen
g ____________ knight	**h** ____________ stepsister	**i** ____________ merchant
j ____________ servant	**k** ____________ woodcutter	**l** ____________ wand
m ____________ dragon	**n** ____________ castle	**o** ____________ giant

Dictionary search

There are some words in traditional tales that we don't use much any more. Do you know the meaning of these old words? If not, look them up in your dictionary.

damsel	courtier	minstrel	jester	charger	tailor	cobbler	moat

Read and learn

You might have seen the film *Shrek*, If so, use your knowledge of the story to work out the meanings of the words in **bold**. Then do activities 1 and 2.

Even if you have not seen the film, you can work out the meanings by using the clues in the text. Don't just look at the words immediately before and after; sometimes you will find the clues two or three sentences away.

The film *Shrek* is about a big green ogre. Beneath his scary **exterior**, Shrek is a very mild-mannered creature who only wants a quiet life. He has lived **contentedly** alone in a stinky, dark swamp for a very long time. However, his happy isolation is **disrupted** when the midget king from the neighbouring kingdom, Lord Farquaad, **banishes** all fairytale characters from his land to Shrek's swamp.

Shrek agrees to an offer that Lord Farquaad makes to him. He will clear out the swamp of the **pesky** creatures if Shrek rescues a princess called Fiona from a fiery **keep** which is guarded by a **fearsome** fire-breathing dragon. But it turns out that Farquaad only wants the princess rescued so he can marry her and become king of her parents' land.

Shrek manages to **fulfil** his part of the bargain, with the help of his trusty **side-kick**, Donkey, but he starts to fall for his damsel in **distress**. She is tough, strong and funny, and definitely not in love with the villain, Farquaad. However, Fiona has an astonishing secret which emerges in the final scenes. I can't tell you the ending, but it makes the film's point that beauty is only skin-deep.

Do you know this word?

A ***parody*** is a book or film that makes a joke of the style or topics of other books or films. It is the same as a *spoof* or a *send-up*. It can be both a noun and verb. For example:

*The film 'Shrek' is a **parody** of the fairytale genre. It makes fun of typical fairytale characters and plots.*

1 Circle the word that best gives the meaning of each word as it is used in the text.

a	exterior	i	exit	ii	outside	iii	face
b	contentedly	i	happily	ii	quietly	iii	unhappily
c	disrupted	i	disturbed	ii	stopped	iii	improved
d	banishes	i	kills	ii	sends away	iii	takes
e	pesky	i	little	ii	fairy	iii	annoying
f	keep	i	stay	ii	guardian	iii	tower
g	fearsome	i	frightened	ii	frightening	iii	fearless
h	fulfil	i	complete	ii	exchange	iii	agree
i	side-kick	i	enemy	ii	assistant	iii	brother
j	distress	i	disturbance	ii	unhappiness	iii	dress

2 Look up any other words you didn't know.

Puzzle

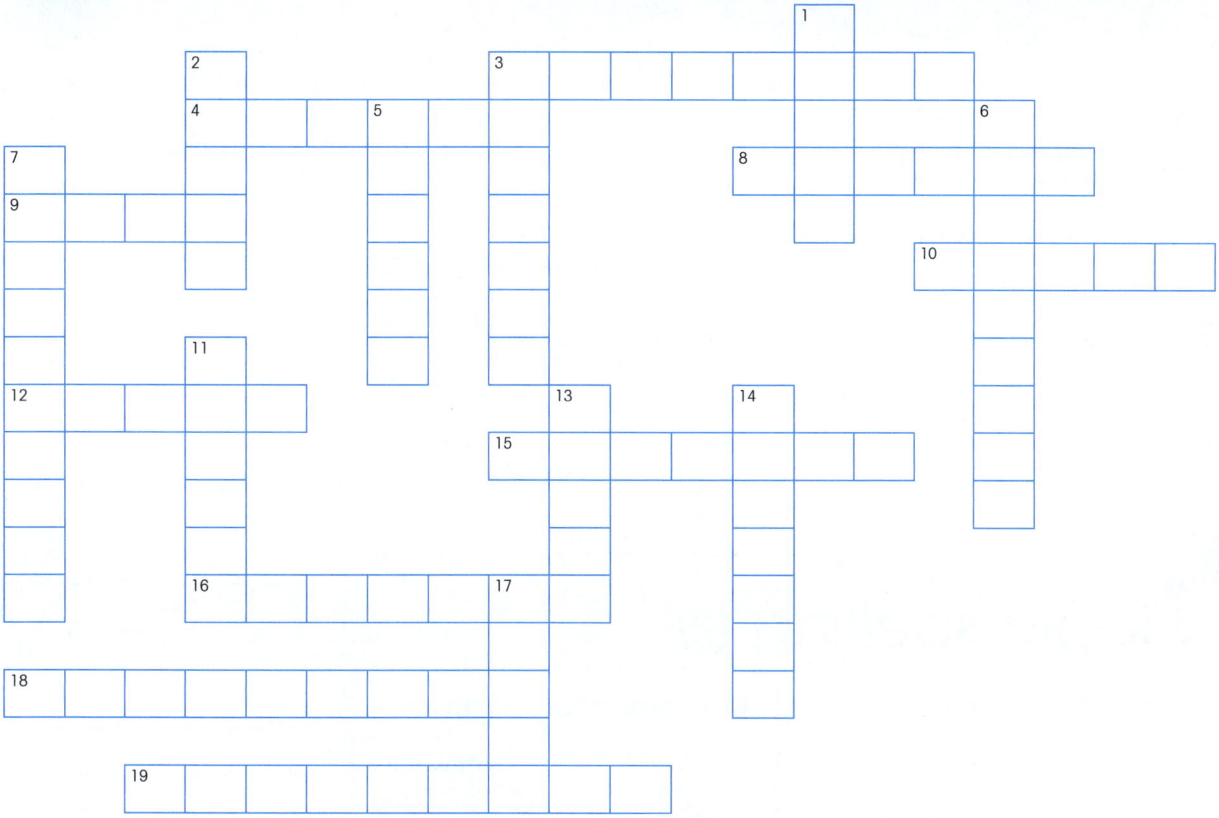

Across

3. Sounds like it has something to do with hands, but it doesn't. (8)
4. One of the main jobs of 11 down. (6)
8. Plural of hero. (6)
9. Ugly and enormous. (4)
10. Soft and silent. (5)
12. A huge ***-ant***. (5)
15. The nastiest character in the story. (7)
16. The knight rode all __________ the night. (7)
18. The one you like the most. (9)
19. Any person in a story. (9)

Down

1. Most castles have at least one of these. (5)
2. Nasty. (5)
3. The most important female in the story. (7)
5. How would you like to live in one of these? (6)
6. Pretty, attractive. (9)
7. The opposite of timid. (10)
11. Often rides a white horse. (6)
13. Rhymes with something you scratch. (5)
14. The way fairytales usually end. (7)
17. Another word for visitor. (5)

Your turn to write

Retell the story of a fairytale you know well. It might be one that scares you, amuses you or makes you cry. If you know traditional tales from another country, you might like to retell one of these. Begin by saying which story you are retelling and why. Then tell the main parts of the story—the plot—and what happens to the most important characters.

Remember to do a rough draft first and then revise and edit your work, before writing it out again.

☞Answers on pages 148–149

8 Water, water, everywhere

Quick fun

Can you unscramble the five oceans of the world?

1. TLNAACIT _ _ _ _ _ _ _ _ _
2. CRIATC _ _ _ _ _ _
3. CIAFPCI _ _ _ _ _ _ _
4. NNIIDA _ _ _ _ _ _
5. RETHUSON _ _ _ _ _ _ _ _ _

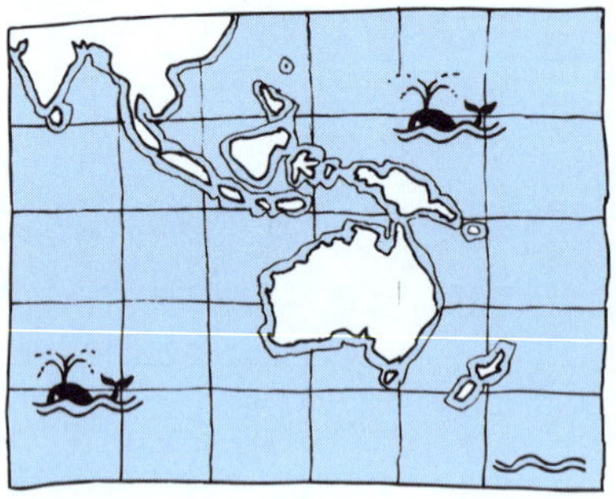

Topic spelling list

stream	tidal
creek	fountain
river	lagoon
swamp	billabong
oceanic	shallow
marine	aquatic
coral	torrent
current	torrential
liquid	tributary
dilute	harbour

Brainstretching strategy

Give yourself a challenge when learning spelling lists. See if you can write the whole list from memory (in any order).

You'll be concentrating so hard on remembering the words that you will automatically get the spelling right.

Use the words from the **Topic spelling list** and then try out this strategy. How did you go?

Word scramble

Which words from the **Topic spelling list** are scrambled below?

1. ATCIUQA ______________
2. NUTNIAOF ______________
3. CACEOIN ______________
4. NOGOLA ______________
5. ROBURAH ______________
6. TTLANEIRRO ______________
7. BBGONALIL ______________
8. TUBAIRTYR ______________

Use this space to write out your topic words the first time. Use your own paper for extra practice.

____

Rewrite here those you had most trouble with.

____

Fill in the gaps

Fill in the gaps with words from the **Topic Spelling list** You might need to add ***ed*** or ***s***.

1. Swimming in rivers can be dangerous, especially if there is a strong ________________.
2. The ________________ in the Great Barrier Reef may die if ________________ temperatures increase.
3. ________________ means relating to the sea. It comes from *mare*—Latin for *sea*.
4. Tsunamis are often called ________________ waves, but they have nothing to do with tides.
5. We ________________ the mixture with water to make it weaker.
6. Medicine is usually put into ________________ form for small children.
7. Our school swimming carnival was at the local ________________ centre.
8. '________________' is an Aboriginal Australian word for *waterhole*.
9. A ________________ is an area of ________________ water separated from the sea or a lake by low land.
10. People often throw coins into a ________________ for good luck.
11. A ________________ is a river, stream or ________________ which joins into a larger river. It *contributes* its water to the river.

11 The rain was absolutely ________________, drenching us to our skins.

12 Sydney has one of the finest, deepest ________________ in the world.

Killer words

Study the words and tips and then write them without looking back.

depth	Remember *dee**p*** and you won't forget the ***p***.	________________
width	Remember *wi**d**e* and you won't forget the ***d***.	________________
dangerous	Say *DANG-ER-OUS* and you'll remember the ***e***.	________________
appear	Remember the double ***p***: a ***p**ear* with an extra ***p***.	________________
disappear	If you get *appear* right, you'll have no trouble.	________________

Use the first three **Killer words** in one sentence. Make your sentence about a word from the **Topic spelling list**.

____

____

____

Now use the last two **Killer words** in one sentence. Again, make it about a word from the **Topic spelling list**.

____

____

Looking at … short o sound spelt *a*

The **short o** sound is mostly spelt with an **o**, e.g. c**o**ral, t**o**rrent. However, after a ***w*** sound and a ***kw*** sound (spelt ***qu***) it is usually spelt ***a***, e.g. *sw**a**mp, aqu**a**tic*. Exceptions are *w**o**bble, w**o**mbat* and *sw**o**t*.

1. Look up any words below that you don't understand. Then learn the words, taking notice of the patterns. Ask your parents or a friend to test your spelling.

squash	swat	swab	swap	waft	watt	wadding
wash	what	wan	want	was	watch	squad
quarry	squat	squabble	wallop	wander	wattle	quadrant
squalid	squatter	swaddle	warrant	twaddle	wallow	squadron

2. Which word from the list means:

a a measure of electricity? ____________ b stupid talk? ____________

c padding? ____________ d argue or fight? ____________

e dirty? ____________ f a kind of tree? ____________

g the past tense of *is*? ____________ h hit hard? ____________

i walk without direction? ____________ j flatten? ____________

k exchange? ____________ l float? ____________

3. Use the pattern to help you write a word for the following.

a An insect similar to a bee. W _ _ _ b A kind of water bird. S W _ _

c Argue. Q U _ _ _ _ _ d A marsh or mangrove. S W _ _ _

e How we eat food. S W _ _ _ _ _ f An object that can be magic. W _ _ _

Proofreading

Can you fix the spelling errors in this research report?

Our group found out some amazing facts about watter.

- Although we call our planit Earth, it is realy one huge osheanik ball.
- More than 70% of the Earth's surface is coverd by osheans.
- The spin of the Earth creates curents that distribute worm and cold watter around the globe.
- The average deth of ocens is four kilometres.
- The Pacfic covers a larger areea than all the contnents put together.
- Streems and rivvers shape the Earth's surface by wearing away the rock they flow over. The Colorado River has taken millions of yers to cut out the Grand Canyon in the USA.

Did you know?

The ocean is blue because water absorbs colours at the opposite end of the spectrum from blue, such as reds and oranges. It is NOT blue because it reflects the blue sky. On an overcast day, the ocean is still blue. The colour can also depend on algae, mud and sand in the water.

Vocabulary power

In English, there are many words with similar meanings (**synonyms**). However, there is usually a slight difference in meaning or in the way the words are used.

1 Look at the verbs below. We use all of these to talk about **adding water or liquid**. Divide the words into the four groups shown. Use your dictionary if you need to.

wet	slosh	drench	dampen	water	plunge
drown	soak	flood	drizzle	pour	moisten
immerse	submerge	spray	bathe	inundate	deluge

Adding small amounts of water	**Adding some water (medium amount)**
Adding large amounts of water	**Completely covering in water**

2 Choose one of the words above to use in these sentences. There may be more than one possibility. Add ***s***, ***ed*** or ***ing*** if needed.

a She ________________ the cloth before she wiped down the kitchen bench.

b You need to ________________ the tablecloth in water to get the stain out.

c The village was completely ________________ by the floodwaters.

d She ________________ her burning hands in the cold water.

e ________________ the liquid into this bottle.

f Mum let us go outside to play because it was only ________________.

g ________________ me with the hose. I'm baking hot.

3 Some words **sound like the action they describe**. For example, *slosh* sounds like a lot of water moving around. These words are called **onomatopoeic words**.

Look at these other **onomatopoeic** words for water. Draw lines to match them to the right picture. There might be more than one way to do this.

splash	squelch	squish
plop	drip	gush
slop	burble	
gurgle	slurp	

a

b

c

d

e

f

g

h

i

j

4 Choose five of the onomatopoeic words above to use in sentences. You could write about the pictures or something else. Use your own paper.

5 What other onomatopoeic words do you know? They might be about the sounds of water, machines, animals or other things.

Read and learn

When we read poems, we often have to work hard to work out the meanings of the lines.

Read these three water poems a few times. Try to imagine the scenes in your head. Then answer questions **1–8**. Circle the answers.

The Sea
by Lilith Norman

Deep glass-green seas
chew rocks
with their green-glass jaws.
But little waves
creep in
and nibble softly at the edges.

The Tide in the River
by Eleanor Farjeon

The tide in the river,
The tide in the river,
The tide in the river runs deep,
I saw a shiver
Pass over the river
As the tide turned in its sleep.

Lake Monger
by William Hart-Smith

On Lake Monger a black swan
makes of its neck an interrogation-mark
punctuating a sentence of ducks.

1. What is 'The Sea' about?
   - **a** when the sea meets the shore
   - **b** a river going into the sea
   - **c** the deepest part of the sea

2. In 'The Sea', which human activity does the poet compare the water's action to?
   - **a** running
   - **b** eating
   - **c** talking

3. 'The Sea' describes
   - **a** big waves.
   - **b** little waves.
   - **c** both big and little waves.

4. What is 'The Tide in the River' about?
   - **a** high tide in the river
   - **b** low tide in the river
   - **c** the change in the tide

5. In 'The Tide in the River', what do you think the poet means by the words 'I saw the shiver'?
   - **a** a change on the surface of the water
   - **b** waves on the river
   - **c** the water getting lower

6. In 'Lake Monger', what does the 'interrogation-mark' refer to?
   - **a** the swan's call
   - **b** the shape of the swan's neck
   - **c** a sign the swan gives to the ducks

7. In 'Lake Monger', what does the 'sentence' refer to?
   - **a** a line of ducks on the water
   - **b** a group of ducks on the water
   - **c** ducks flying in the air

8. Can you see in your head a picture of the scene each poet paints? Yes / No (*circle*)

   Which picture is the clearest to you? ___________

Puzzle

Can you work out these cryptic clues to get a word from the unit?

- **a** Rhymes with **mountain**. ____________________
- **b** Past tense of **swim** plus another letter. ____________________
- **c** A form of **will** plus ***ow*** (not deep). ____________________
- **d** Shares three letters with **fluid** and means much the same. ____________________
- **e** Sounds like a **dried berry** but spelt differently. ____________________
- **f** Take the **sub** from an ocean vessel to get a word meaning about the sea. ____________________
- **g** Rhymes with **flute**. ____________________
- **h** The biggest ocean; also a word meaning **calm**. ____________________
- **i** This ocean gives a **direction**. ____________________
- **j** A noun meaning **how wide**. ____________________
- **k** Opposite of **appear**. ____________________
- **l** **Very pale** (starts with ***w***, has only three letters). ____________________
- **m** If you **swat** a fly, you will also do this to it. (begins with ***squ***). ____________________

Your turn to write

Write a poem about water. For example, you could choose the ocean, the sea, the seashore, a river, a stream or a billabong. Choose something you feel strongly about, perhaps a watery place you feel happy in, or one you are afraid of. Try to use words from **Vocabulary power** to describe the scene. Use your own paper. You might like to illustrate your poem as well.

☞ Answers on pages 149–150

9 Describing people

Quick fun

When we describe the way people look, we describe their *features*. How many words can you make from FEATURES? There are at least 20! Use your own paper.

Topic spelling list

pretty	attractive
slender	pleasant
plump	crooked
olive-skinned	ordinary
blonde	charming
curly-haired	lovely
frizzy	gorgeous
straight	extremely
scarred	rather
freckles	similar

Stunning strategy

Breaking words into syllables helps you to avoid missing out letters in longer words, e.g. *ORD-IN-AR-Y, AV-ER-AGE* (one vowel sound per syllable).

Break up the words from the **Topic spelling list** into syllables and learn them using the LOOK-SAY-COVER-WRITE-CHECK method.

Use this space to write out your topic words the first time. Use your own paper for extra practice.

Rewrite here those you had most trouble with.

Fill in the gaps

Fill in the gaps with words from the **Topic spelling list**. There may be more than one possible answer.

1. The robber's face was badly ____________ and looked ____________ dangerous. However, he had a quite ____________ way of speaking.
2. His mouth was quite ____________, but he had a very ____________ nose.
3. I hate my curly hair because it always goes ____________ in the rain.
4. The model had perfectly ____________, ____________ hair, which reached to her very ____________ waist.

5. The woman's ______________ face hid her vicious cruelty.
6. My brother gets at least fifty more ______________ every time he goes out in the sun.
7. Even though my father is ______________, he has to be careful not to burn.
8. The bag-snatcher had a very round, ______________ face and a very large stomach.
9. My grandma is ______________ short and my grandpa is ______________ tall, so my father turned out medium height.
10. Stop putting on that make-up. You look ______________ already.
11. Everyone says I am very ______________ to my brother and sister in looks but very different in temperament.

Killer words

Study the words and tips and then write them without looking back.

hasn't	Don't write it as it sounds. Remember: ***n't*** NOT ***ent***.	______________
wearing	Remember: you ***wear*** an ***ear****ring*.	______________
weight	Learn *weight* and *height* together with number *eight*.	______________
height		______________
different	Break it into syllables to get the middle **e**.	______________

Use the **Killer words** in this sentence.

Her ______________ and ______________ haven't changed much, and she ______________ been ______________ anything very ______________, but somehow she looks a totally new person.

Proofreading

Can you check the spelling of this newspaper article before it goes to print?

SUPERMARKET HOLD-UP

Police are looking for two men who held up a supermarket in Milson's Bay at around 7 p.m. last night. The older man was waring a mask, so police are uncertain about his facial feetures. However, he was decsribed by witnesses as of avrage hight and weght with frizy dark hair, and probly olive-skined. He wore an unnusual multi-coloured coat and extremeley baggy trousers.

The younger man was decsribed as fair-skined, with strait red hair and freckels. He was wering old jeans and a yellow T-shirt.

One witness who spoke to the man said 'The younger man had a very plesant voice and a rathar charmming smile. He didn't look dangrous at all.'

Police are asking the public to come forward if they have information about the two suspects.

Looking at … *ur* words

The ***ur* sound** is very tricky because it is spelt in many ways. One **common spelling** is ***ur*** (*c**ur**l*), but the ***ur*** sound is also spelt ***er*** (*h**er**, c**er**tain*) and ***ir*** (*b**ir**d, f**ir**m*).

The best idea is to learn the spellings of common words and use your dictionary when in doubt.

1 Look at these common ***ur*** words. Learn them and ask a parent or friend to test your spelling.

burn	church	curl	curve	surf
turn	absurd	burglar	further	gurgle
murder	murmur	occur	purse	purchase
disturb	surface	surgeon	surname	turkey
urban	urchin	purple	sturdy	curt

2 Complete the ***ur*** puzzle with words from the list, using the clues below. Try to do this without looking back at the spellings.

a	U	R						A city area.
b		U	R					The outside part of something.
c			U	R				A place of worship.
d				U	R			Ridiculous.
e					U	R		Interrupt.
f						U	R	Speak softly.
g					U	R		Happen, take place.
h				U	R			Strong and solid.
i			U	R				A kind of bird.
j		U	R					Farther.
k	U	R						An uncared for street child.
l		U	R					A doctor who operates.

3 Now choose words from the list to use in these sentences.

a Write your ____________________ here, and sign at the bottom of the page.

b The little brook ____________________ down the valley.

c I was lost. I just didn't know which way to ____________________.

d I could not describe the ____________________, but I would know him if I saw him.

e The road ____________________ sharply towards the left and then straightened up again.

f I left my ____________________ at home so I couldn't pay for all my ____________________.

Looking at … comparing people and things

We often compare people or things to others when describing them. For example:
Maria is shorter than Josie. Her hair is curlier and her face is more freckled. Tessa is the shortest. Her hair is the curliest and her face is the most freckled.

Follow these rules to compare correctly:
- add **er** and **est** to adjectives of one syllable, e.g. *short*, *shorter*, *shortest*
- double the last letter before adding **er** and **est** for adjectives with a short vowel + one consonant, e.g. *fat*, *fatter*, *fattest*
- change the ***y*** to ***i*** before adding **er** and **est** for adjectives ending in ***y***, e.g. *curly*, *curlier*, *curliest*
- use **more** and **most** for adjectives with more than one syllable, e.g. *freckled*, *more freckled*, *most freckled*.

Fill in the chart with the correct forms of the adjectives. The first one has been done for you.

	Comparing two people or things	**Comparing more than two people or things**
skinny	skinnier	skinniest
sturdy		
pleasant		
pretty		
attractive		
frizzy		
charming		
straight		
plump		
red		
blonde		

Vocabulary power

1 There are many **vivid and precise adjectives** we can use to **describe people**. You should try to use these instead of always using the same ones, such as *big*, *small*, *nice*, etc. Use your dictionary to find the meanings of these words.

a	dainty	______________	**b**	hideous	______________
c	dapper	______________	**d**	lithe	______________
e	elegant	______________	**f**	rugged	______________
g	ungainly	______________	**h**	willowy	______________
i	ruddy	______________	**j**	exquisite	______________
k	cherubic	______________	**l**	striking	______________

2 Which of the words above might you use to describe

a a ballet dancer? ____________

b a farmer? ____________

c an ogre? ____________

d a well-dressed man? ____________

e a female model? ____________

f a sportsman? ____________

g a toddler? ____________

Note: There is more than one answer possible.

3 Make up five **true** sentences about your friends using the words in this unit. Be kind, won't you! Use your own paper.

Read and learn

Descriptions 'paint pictures' in our minds of characters and scenes. Sometimes they contain unusual words or phrases, especially if the book was written long ago.

Read this extract from a classic children's book, *Anne of Green Gables* by LM Montgomery. Think carefully about the possible meaning of the words in **bold** as you read.

The extract describes the first meeting of an old man, Matthew, and a young girl whom he and his wife have adopted. At the time of the meeting, he is expecting a boy, not a girl.

> An ordinary observer would have seen this: a child of about eleven, **garbed** in a very short, very tight, very ugly dress of yellowish white **wincey**. She wore a faded brown sailor hat and beneath the hat, extending down her back, were two **braids** of very thick, **decidedly** red hair. Her face was small, white and thin, also much freckled; her mouth was large and so were her eyes that looked green in some lights and moods, and grey in others.
>
> So far the ordinary observer; an extraordinary observer might have seen that the chin was very pointed and **pronounced**; that the big eyes were full of **spirit and vivacity**; that the mouth was sweet-lipped and expressive; that the forehead was broad and full; in short, our **discerning** extraordinary observer might have concluded that no **commonplace** soul inhabited the body of this stray woman-child of whom shy Matthew Cuthbert was so **ludicrously** afraid.

1 Circle the answer which best gives the meaning of each word or expression as it is used in the text.

a	garbed	i	dressed	ii	decorated
b	wincey	i	small	ii	a kind of fabric
c	braids	i	plaits	ii	ribbons
d	decidedly	i	consciously	ii	definitely
e	pronounced	i	spoken	ii	obvious
f	spirit	i	energy	ii	ghostly look
g	vivacity	i	liveliness	ii	doubt
h	discerning	i	typical	ii	observant
i	commonplace	i	ordinary	ii	extraordinary
j	ludicrously	i	surprisingly	ii	ridiculously

2 Which paragraph describes what a person would see if they looked beneath the surface appearance of the girl? ________

3 If you like, draw a picture of the girl described as you now imagine her.

Do you know these expressions?

The phrase ***to look a million dollars*** means to look attractive and well-dressed.

The phrase ***to look like something the cat dragged in*** means the opposite—to look unattractive and badly or oddly dressed. For example:

*She **looked a million dollars** on her wedding day.*

*She **looked like something the cat dragged in**, but none of us knew how to tell her.*

Puzzle

Try this no-clue crossword. All the words are from the **Topic spelling list** or **Killer words**.

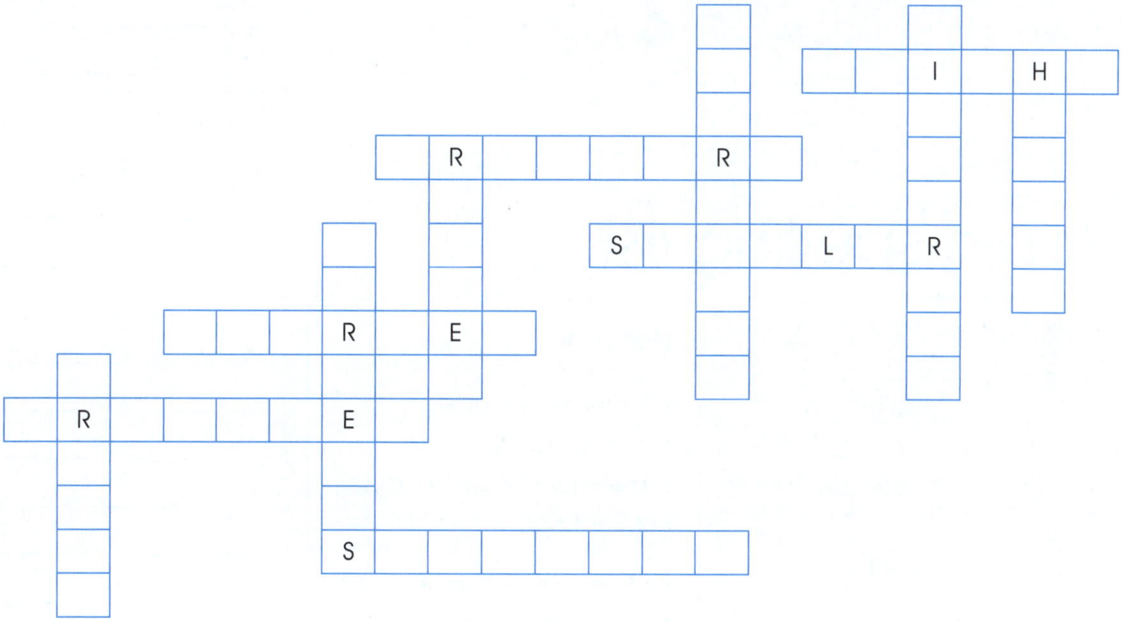

Your turn to write

Choose one of the following tasks. Do your writing on your own paper, but make sure you do a rough draft first. Revise and edit your work, and then write it out again.

1 Imagine one of your friends is coming to stay at your house. Your mum has not met your friend before, but she is picking him or her up from the station. You can't be there, so you write a description to help your mum recognise your friend.

OR

2 Write a short newspaper article describing a person the police are seeking for a robbery in your area. Begin by briefly saying what happened, when and where.

OR

3 Describe someone in your family.

☞ Answers on pages 150–151

10 In the country

Quick fun

Can you unscramble these 'country' words from previous units? One or two letters from each word have been put in the right place to help you.

1. UNMOINTA M _ _ _ _ _ _ N
2. WAMSP _ _ _ _ P
3. ILLBOABNG B _ _ _ _ B _ _ _
4. DERTES D _ _ _ _ _
5. CEKRE _ R _ _ _
6. VRIER _ _ V _ _
7. SEAMTR _ _ _ _ _ M
8. LOONAG _ _ G _ _ _

Topic spelling list

field
range
cliff
forest
paddock
meadow
landscape
scenery
nature
natural

flora
fauna
spacious
rural
village
national park
wilderness
environment
magnificent
spectacular

Hot hint

Write the word quickly: the correct spelling sometimes comes to mind automatically.

Write the words from the **Topic spelling list** using the LOOK-SAY-COVER-WRITE-CHECK method. Try to write the letters of each word quickly.

Use this space to write out your topic words the first time. Use your own paper for extra practice.

Rewrite here those you had most trouble with.

Fill in the gaps

Fill in the gaps with words from the **Topic spelling list**. There may be more than one word possible. Add **s** if needed.

1. The Great Dividing ________ forms a barrier between the east coast of Australia and the inland.
2. It can be rather frightening to walk through a dark ________.
3. A '________' is a fenced area for farm animals, but in Australia the word can be used to describe any grassy ________.
4. The ________ of Tasmania varies every few miles.
5. Country and state emblems usually include native ________ and ________.
6. The waves lashed against the towering ________.
7. We bought supplies for the expedition at a tiny ________ near the entrance to the ________ ________.
8. The only way to see the ________ area of south-west Tasmania is by aeroplane or helicopter.
9. We should take care of the ________ for future generations.
10. City people like to holiday in the country because it takes them closer to ________.
11. The view from the top of the mountain was ________.
12. '________' is the opposite of *urban*.
13. It is so much more ________ in the country, and some of the scenery is ________.

Killer words

Study the words and tips and then write them without looking back.

quiet	Remember: ET (the extraterrestrial) was very *quiET*.	________
quite	If you remember the other *quiet*, you'll get this right.	________
though	A horrible word! Write it out 10 times.	________
although	Do the same for *although*.	________
instead	Learn with *head* and *bread*.	________
picture	Use a spelling pronunciation to help.	________

Use the **Killer words** in three sentences: two words in each sentence.

____

____

____

Looking at … *soft g* and *dge* words

Always put **ge** for the sound ***j*** at the end of a word, e.g. *villa**ge***, *ran**ge***. We never end a word with the letter ***j***. The soft ***g*** for the ***j*** sound also occurs within words before **e**, ***i*** or ***y***, e.g. **ge***rm*, **gi***nger*, **gy***m*.

huge	gem	dangerous	gigantic	magic
large	germ	generous	image	gymnastics
lunge	genius	angel	margin	gypsy
geography	religion	agent	origin	Egypt

1 Which word from the list means:

a kind? ____________ b picture? ____________

c virus? ____________ d vast, enormous? ____________

e the study of the earth? ____________ f a country? ____________

g a brilliant person? ____________ h big? ____________

i suddenly move forward? ____________ j a wandering race of people? ____________

2 Use the pattern to help you write a soft ***g*** word for the following. (These are not from the list.)

a You might use this on your hair. _ _ L b Soft and quiet. _ _ _ T L _

c Very, very sad. T _ _ _ _ C d A plant and also a hair colour. _ I N _ _ R

e The study of rocks. _ E O _ O G _ f A doctor who operates. S U _ _ E O _

g To see in your mind. _ M A _ I N _ h A place to get fit. _ _ M

3 After a short vowel sound, the ***j*** sound is sometimes spelt **dge**, e.g. *bri**dge***, *e**dge***, *do**dge***. What **dge** words am I thinking of?

a A tasty sweet. _ _ D G E b An important person in court. _ _ D G E

c Push gently. _ _ D G E d Something used in the snow. _ _ _ D G E

e A mark or blur. _ _ _ D G E f A triangular-shaped piece. _ _ D G E

g A bush like a fence. _ _ D G E h Known information. _ _ _ _ _ _ D G E

i Breakfast. _ _ _ _ _ D G E j To walk with a heavy tread. _ _ _ D G E

4 These words have **dg** in the middle. What are they?

a A useful small tool. _ _ D G _ _ b Can't sit still. _ _ D G _ _

c A dwarf. _ _ D G _ _ d A saving plan. _ _ D G _ _

Proofreading

Can you correct the spelling errors in this camp diary?

We camped at the ejj of a huje forrest. The senery was absolutely spectular, but we were far too nervous to care much about it. The clifs we had earlyer thort magnificent, we now saw as threatening. Altho we had relly wanted to experiense naytcher, somehow it did not seem so important now that we were lost and alone. We would probly not go much firther than the padoks at the end of our town from now on. The only fawna we wanted to see were our pet cats and dogs. We knew there was a small vilage about ten miles away and we desided we wuld aim for that the next day. We tried to settel down to sleep, but before too long the quite was broken by a distirbing rustle.

Vocabulary power

1 Some words **often go together** in English. Can you find three adjectives from the box which are often used with the nouns **a–g** to **describe** the **scenery**?

steep	mighty	rocky	green	open	unspoilt	swollen
dramatic	winding	bleak	towering	desolate	dense	grassy
deep	rugged	pretty	barren	quaint	picturesque	dark

a cliffs ________ ________ ________

b fields ________ ________ ________

c forest ________ ________ ________

d village ________ ________ ________

e landscape ________ ________ ________

f wilderness ________ ________ ________

g river ________ ________ ________

2 All the words below are used to describe beautiful scenery, but their syllables are jumbled up. Can you unscramble them?

breath**ful**	dram**acular**	spect**atic**	stun**ful**
sup**ous**	delight**taking**	glori**erb**	wonder**ning**

________ ________ ________ ________

________ ________ ________ ________

3 Use the words above and in the **Topic spelling list** to write sentences about three **real** places you know, either here or overseas. Use your own paper.

Read and learn

Descriptions we read in stories are often quite difficult to understand. The writer might use unusual words and images to paint a picture, and you may have to read a section a few times to fully understand it.

Read this description from a famous Australian children's novel, and circle the correct answers.

> It was late in the afternoon of the third day, and in a cloud of thick dust the riders were hurrying along the road towards Atholton. Ahead they could see the scattered roofs of the little township, showing white among the trees; but everything was obscured by the dust that swirled and eddied, now tearing away before them in a cloud sixty feet high, or seeming to stand still all around them, blinding any vision for more than a few yards. Behind, a leaden sky glowered through the dust-clouds, or was revealed darkly purple, when they rose for an instant to swirl and scurry, and grow dense again, as the shrieking wind came in a fresh gust.
>
> From *Norah of Billabong* by Mary Grant Bruce.

1. What does the phrase 'scattered roofs' tell you about Atholton?
   - **a** nobody lived there
   - **b** the roofs had been blown off by the dust
   - **c** the town was spread out

2. What is the best way to describe the dust's movement?
   - **a** moving quickly and wildly
   - **b** moving slowly and calmly
   - **c** not moving at all

3. The word 'obscured' means
   - **a** destroyed. **b** covered. **c** hidden.

4. What colour was the sky when seen through the clouds?
   - **a** dark purple **b** dark grey **c** white

5. What are the riders experiencing?
   - **a** a dust storm **b** an electrical storm **c** a hurricane

6. Which word best describes the mood or atmosphere created by the writer?
   - **a** threatening **b** mysterious **c** depressing

Do you know this word?

The adjective **idyllic** means happy, peaceful and simple. For example:

*The villagers led an **idyllic** life until the superhighway was built nearby.*

Puzzle

1. Can you work out these words from the **Topic spelling list**?
   - **a** _ _ ☐ _ _ A place to play sport, as well as something often seen in the country.
   - **b** _ _ ☐ _ _ A place to shoot rifles, as well as a string of mountains.
   - **c** ☐ _ _ _ _ _ _ A tiny town.

d _ _ ☐ _ _ The edge of the land.

e _ _ ☐ _ _ Relating to country not city areas.

f _ _ ☐ _ _ Plants of a particular area.

g _ _ _ ☐ _ Animals of a particular area.

h ☐ _ _ _ _ _ The same as option **a** above (but not a place for sport).

i _ _ ☐ _ _ _ _ What you can see around you.

j ☐ _ _ _ _ _ _ Not artificial.

k _ _ _ _ _ _ _ _ _ _ ☐ Extraordinarily good.

Now write the letters in the boxes below to make a word that covers all of these.

☐ ☐ ☐ ☐ ☐ ☐ ☐ ☐ ☐ ☐ ☐

2 Can you use these cryptic clues to work out words from the **Killer words** and **Looking at ...** sections.

a Could be a photograph. ☐ _ ☐ _ _ _ _

b Rhymes with *bread* and *head.* _ _ _ _ _ _ ☐

c A school subject. _ _ _ _ _ _ ☐ _ _

d The countryside is not always safe. _ _ _ ☐ _ _ _ _ ☐

e Something to keep you fit. _ _ _ _ ☐ _ _ _ _ _

f A **gh** word that means something like *but.* _ ☐ _ _ _ _ _ _

g Shh! _ _ _ ☐ _

Now write the letters from the boxes and unscramble them to get a nine-letter word from the topic list.

It begins with ***l*** and ends in **e**. _ _ _ _ _ _ _ _ _ → __________

Your turn to write

Look at the picture and imagine you are there. Write a description of the scene as a diary entry. Try to use words from the unit. Do your writing on your own paper, but make sure you do a rough draft first. Revise and edit your work, and then write it out again.

Answers on page 151

Review 2

Now let's see what you remember of the words you learnt in Units 6–10.

Step 1 Look at each group of words in the test to revise the spellings.

Step 2 Cover the five words up and test yourself (column 2). Try to do all five words in one go.

Step 3 Write your score out of 5 in the box. If you got any words wrong, go back and study them again.

Step 4 If possible, ask someone to test you on the words later—an hour or even a day later (column 3).

Test 1

Study	Test yourself	Test with another person
ancient period warrior reign rebellion	/5	/5
battle peaceful kingdom pioneer emperor	/5	/5
conquer history colony government warn	/5	/5
through during century known discovered	/5	/5
always towards almost heroine handsome	/5	/5
heroes princess wicked rescue villain	/5	/5
	Total score = out of 30	Total score = out of 30

Test 2

Study	Test yourself	Test with another person
castle cruel knight dungeon ogre	/5	/5
courageous character favourite happily beautiful	/5	/5
swamp oceanic marine coral current	/5	/5
liquid dilute fountain lagoon billabong	/5	/5
shallow aquatic torrential tributary harbour	/5	/5
depth width dangerous disappear squash	/5	/5
	Total score = out of 30	Total score = out of 30

Test 3

Study	Test yourself	Test with another person
swap pretty wander olive-skinned squadron	/5	/5
frizzy straight scarred freckles attractive	/5	/5
pleasant crooked ordinary lovely gorgeous	/5	/5
extremely rather similar hasn't wearing	/5	/5
weight height different absurd burglar	/5	/5
field range cliff murder murmur	/5	/5
	Total score = out of 30	Total score = out of 30

Test 4

Study	Test yourself	Test with another person
further gurgle forest paddock meadow	/5	/5
landscape scenery nature natural flora	/5	/5
occur fauna spacious village disturb	/5	/5
surface national park wilderness environment magnificent	/5	/5
purchase spectacular rural genius religion	/5	/5
although instead picture image origin	/5	/5
	Total score = out of 30	Total score = out of 30

Which word?

Well done!

1. Everyone ______________ Charlie came to my party. (*except, accept*)
2. I'm not ______________ to go to the carnival. (*aloud, allowed*)
3. She took a ______________ of pie. (*piece, peace*)
4. Go ______________ to the kitchen. (*through, threw*)
5. He's ______________ tall for his age. (*quite, quiet*)
6. I'll bet ______________ still asleep. (*there, they're, their*)
7. Bring ______________ swimmers. (*your, you're*)

☞ Answers on page 151

11 Moving around

Quick fun

Can you change COME to BACK in five moves? And SWIMS to CRAWL in six moves?

C O M E

_ _ _ _ (middle)

_ _ _ _ (look after)

_ _ _ _ (uncovered)

_ _ _ _ (found on a tree)

B A C K

S W I M S

_ _ _ _ _ (gets thinner)

_ _ _ _ _ (shuts with force)

_ _ _ _ _ (a kind of seafood)

_ _ _ _ _ (fingernails of some animals)

_ _ _ _ _ (necks or gullets of birds)

C R A W L

Topic spelling list

hurrying	movement
haste	mobile
crawl	rapidly
wandered	gradually
followed	swiftly
forwards	smoothly
backwards	suddenly
towards	motionless
squirm	velocity
wriggle	accelerate

Dynamic hint

Chanting spellings out loud many times can help you to memorise words. Chant with a good beat to help you remember the rhythm.

It can also help to shout out the most difficult letters. Which letter would you shout out in *accelerate*?

Write out the words from the **Topic spelling list**. Chant the spellings of those you find difficult to remember.

Word scramble

Which words from the **Topic spelling list** are scrambled below?

1. TOMINO ____________
2. DEDERNAW ____________
3. GINYRHRU ____________
4. DILYPAR ____________
5. LYLAURGDA ____________
6. RDWASABCK ____________
7. DEWLOLOF ____________
8. DEDUSYLN

Use this space to write out your topic words the first time. Use your own paper for extra practice.

Rewrite here those you had most trouble with.

Fill in the gaps

Fill in the gaps with words from the **Topic spelling list**. Add endings where needed, e.g. ***ed***, ***ly***, ***ing***.

1. The van ________________ suddenly as the police came closer.
2. The car rocked ________________ and ________________ for a few seconds, then plunged into the gully. The ________________ made the crowd gasp.
3. The competitor began slowly, but ________________ made up speed, and finally won by two seconds.
4. I felt sorry for the worm as it ________________ on the edge of the fishhook.
5. Now we think of a ________________ as a phone, but it actually means *moveable*.
6. The small girl had been ________________ for hours in the bush, but she was not hurt.
7. He was ________________ through his homework so he could go out and play football.
8. The family cheered as the little fellow ________________ unsteadily towards them.
9. The ________________ of the rocket was greater than the speed of sound.
10. The little boy stood ________________ on the big stage, his body paralysed with fear. His teacher moved ________________ towards him and whispered in his ear.
11. 'More ________________, less speed' means the more you hurry, the slower you will be.
12. He spoke so ________________ that no one could work out what he was saying.

Killer words

Study the words and tips and then write them without looking back.

competition	Say the syllables out loud so you won't miss one.	________________
won	This might help: *I **won** on M**on**day*.	________________
nearly	Be *clear* when saying *near* and you'll get it right.	________________
rhythm	This is definitely one for chanting out loud!	________________
stationary	Remember: *the c**ar** was station**ary*** (not moving).	________________

Try to use all the **Killer words** in one sentence. If you can't manage one sentence, make it two.

____

____

____

Looking at … *ir* words

In Unit 9 (p. 56), we looked at one way to spell the ***er*** sound—with ***ur*** as in t***ur***n and h***ur***dle. Here we look at another way—with ***ir*** as in squ***ir***m and th***ir***ty. There is no definite way to know which spelling to use, so it is best to check your dictionary if in doubt.

Look at this list of common ***ir*** words, and write them out in alphabetical order. Remember: if two words begin with the same letter, put them in order of the second letter. If the second letter is the same, put them in order of the third, and so on.

birth	virtue	thirsty	circular	whirl	twirl
swirl	third	stir	sir	shirt	squirt
squirm	girder	mirth	quirky	flirt	firm
firstly	skirmish	skirt	thirty	virgin	fir

Did you notice that ***ir*** occurs more often after certain consonant sounds? Which ones? ______

Looking at … doubling

For words ending in a **short vowel + single consonant**, we **double the last consonant** before adding ***ed***, ***er*** or ***ing***. For example: *hop* → *hopped* → *hopping; travel* → *travelled* → *travelling.*

1 Look at the pictures and write the words. The first letter has been provided for you.

a t ______ (ed)
______ (ing)

b d ______ (er)
______ (ing)

c b ______ (er)
______ (ing)

d q ______ (ed)
______ (ing)

e t ______ (er)
______ (ing)

f j ______ (er)
______ (ing)

2 Would you double the last consonant before adding ***ed***, ***er*** or ***ing*** to these words? Circle yes or no.

a	stamp	yes/no	**b**	crawl	yes/no	**c**	twitch	yes/no	**d**	plod	yes/no
e	fool	yes/no	**f**	slip	yes/no	**g**	pot	yes/no	**h**	omit	yes/no

Proofreading

Can you correct the spelling errors in this short story?

I was in the car with my Mum and Dad on the way to the most important rythmic gymnastics compition of the year. I had nilly wun last year and was determind that this time I would definitly come ferst. The traffic had been terrible all the way and I was getting very worried. Now it was completly stationry. I rocked backwoods and forwoods on my seat, and fiddled with my uniform. Then I started practising my gym movments. Dad told me to stop squrming around. Sudenly, we acelerated. The traffic graduly began to clear. I asked Mum if I could ring Mariella on the mobil and see where she was. 'No', she and Dad shouted with one voice. 'Just sit still. We'll be there in therty seconds.' Well, we did get there in time. And I did win. Dad reckoned it was because I got so much time to practise in the back seat!

Vocabulary power

There are many **vivid and precise verbs** to describe the way people move. You should try using these when writing. They will paint a much clearer picture in your reader's mind than simply using words like *move*, *go*, *come* and *walk*.

1 Look up these words in a good dictionary and write the meaning in your own words. Use your own paper. Even if you think you know them, look them up to get an exact meaning.

saunter	plod	trudge	lumber	swoop
scamper	slither	slouch	scurry	stride
shuffle	amble	prance	toddle	dawdle

2 Now choose one of the words above to describe the way these people and animals might move. There may be more than one possibility.

a A lazy student in trouble. ______________ **b** A bird looking for prey. ______________

c A very tired bushwalker. ______________ **d** A herd of elephants. ______________

e A very old person. ______________ **f** A small animal in the bush. ______________

Read and learn

Read this story extract. It describes a father's attempts to get rid of a pelican which is eating all the fish in the farm dam. As you read, underline all the words you can find which describe movement—of people or the pelican.

At first, the pelican was welcomed. The family would wander down and watch it eat the fish. it would gently glide towards the reeds, dip and lunge with its opened scoop, lift and tilt its head, gulp—and another of Dad's precious fish gone. So began his various schemes to rid the dam of the pelican.

Plan one saw Dad screaming, waving his shirt, jumping up and down. The pelican cruised sedately to the centre of the dam, turned, and stared at the bearded nutter dancing about on the dam wall. The pelican just waited for my father to tire and go away.

Days later, plan two was tried. This one depended not on persuasion, but on intimidation. Dad attacked the pelican with smooth skipping rocks gathered from the creek bed. He hurled them at the pelican, aiming to frighten, not maim. Failure. The pelican didn't lurch into flight; it just drifted quietly into the middle of the dam unruffled, and waited for the nutter hurling missiles to go away.

Plan number three involved the shot-gun. The rusting relic was reclaimed from the rafters in the shed and unwrapped from the decaying sugar bag—a little like an Egyptian mummy undressed after three thousand years. The idea was to blast the air and water around the pelican. Nothing happened. Like the mummy, the gun was dead.

… For three days none of us wandered too far from the house—we knew another *brilliant* plan was about to be activated. 'I don't want anybody near the front dam, I won't be long.' As Dad stomped from the kitchen, the rest of us swapped knowing glances and we all rushed to my bedroom. We knelt, peering over the windowsill.

Dad crawled low, zigzagging commando style, through the oats. The pelican stood on the bank, preening. Mum giggled. Dad reached the reeds, fell on his stomach, and crawled to within fifteen metres of his victim. As he sprang from his starting blocks, the pelican began its take off. The waddle became a run. With wings outstretched and pumping, it reached the water, took three paces and started to lift off. Just then, Dad dived full-length and rugby tackled it. The bird thrashed about. The dam churned with panic as ducks, waders and galahs searched for safety. Dad hung on and squeezed. The pelican's flapping wings delivered left and right hooks and the odd jab and uppercut.

'Oh no,' was all Mum could utter.

Adapted from 'Dad Nil: the Pelican Four' in *Through the Web and Other Stories* by Paul Williams.

How many did you find? There are at least 14.

Read the extract again to properly appreciate the vivid language used to describe the scene.

Do you know these expressions?

All these expressions describe **how fast or slow** a person is moving. How many do you know?

nimble-footed	swift as an arrow	quick as lightning
full speed	like a shot	at a snail's pace
in double-quick time	at a cracking pace	go great guns
by leaps and bounds	hit your stride	drag your feet

Puzzle

Can you complete this crossword with words from the unit?

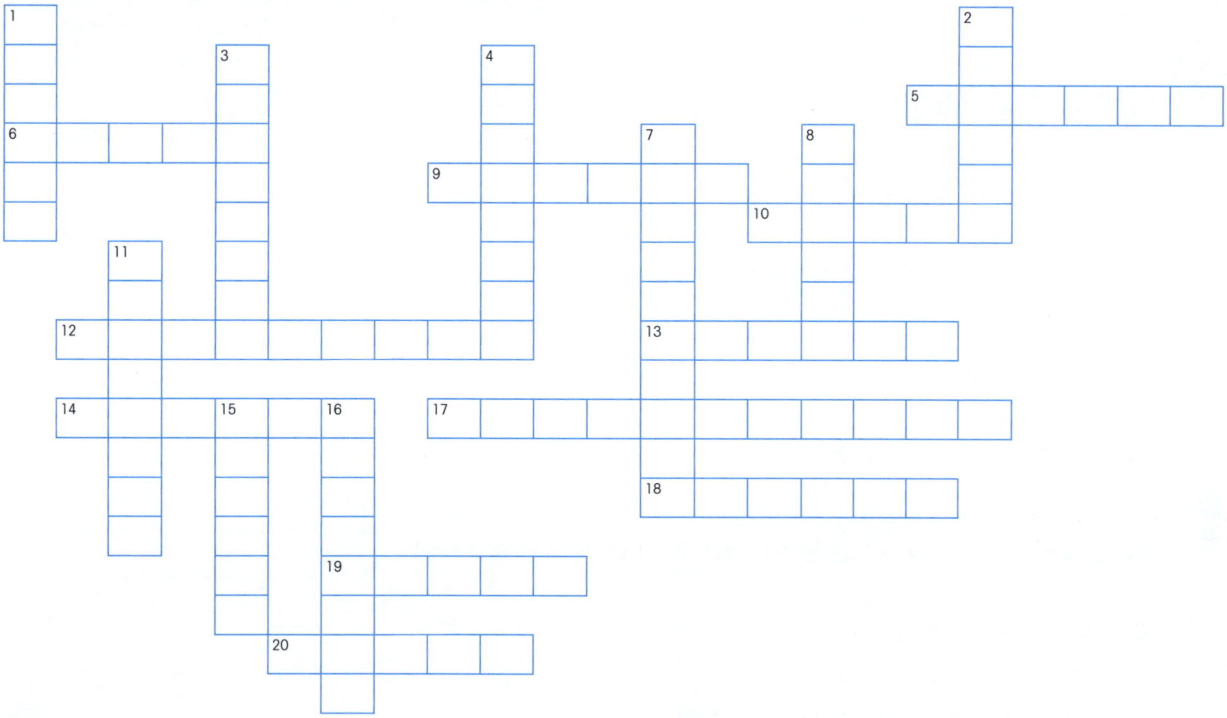

Across

5. Walk in a tired way.
6. A gymnast might do this with a stick and ribbon.
9. A synonym of *movement*.
10. Walk in a relaxed, slow way.
12. An antonym of *suddenly*.
13. A synonym of *almost*.
14. A lost person might do this.
17. A match or fight.
18. Move very quickly; rhymes with *hurry*.
19. Speed of action.
20. An ***ir*** word for *laughter* and *jolliness*.

Down

1. An ***ir*** synonym of *goodness*.
2. Walk with big, confident steps.
3. What did the police do to catch their man? They ____________ him.
4. Another word for *speed*.
7. A synonym of *stationary*.
8. Move in a heavy, laboured way.
11. An antonym of *backwards*.
15. A lazy, slow walk.
16. With a regular, smooth beat.

Your turn to write

Imagine you are at a sports event. There are lots of people doing different things and moving in different ways.

Describe the scene before you, particularly the movements of the competitors and perhaps the crowd too. Try to use some words from the unit, including some of the verbs from **Vocabulary power** and expressions from the **Do you know?** box.

Do your writing on your own paper, but make sure you do a rough draft first. Revise and edit your work, and then write it out again.

☞Answers on pages 152–153

12 Working with maths

Quick fun

Can you work out the answers to these tricky maths puzzles?

Which six-letter word, if you take two letters away, has nine left?

____

Hint: the word spells a number.

How can you take 1 from 19 and get 20?

____

Hint: think about a different way we write numbers—rather old-fashioned.

What five-letter word beginning with **s** gets shorter when you add two letters to it? ______________________________

Hint: it concerns one of the words in the question.

Topic spelling list

amount
average
multiplied
multiplication
addition
subtraction
division
quarter
divide
decrease
total
estimate
percentage
graph
digit
fraction
decimal
equal
minus
plus

Totally top tip

Do crosswords and word puzzles whenever you can. They make you think about common spelling patterns and word meanings. Maths puzzles can do this too.

Write out the words from the **Topic spelling list** using the LOOK-SAY-COVER-WRITE-CHECK method.

Use this space to write out your topic words the first time. Use your own paper for extra practice.

____
____
____
____
____
____
____
____
____
____
____
____
____
____
____
____
____
____
____
____

Rewrite here those you had most trouble with.

____
____
____
____
____
____
____
____
____

Fill in the gaps

Fill in the gaps with words from the **Topic spelling list**. Add ***s*** or ***ed*** if needed.

1. We drew a bar ____________ to show the different ages in our class.
2. In the United States, a ____________ is the common name for 25 cents.
3. 3589 is a four-____________ number.
4. First I ____________ the amount I needed, and then I measured it out exactly.
5. A ____________ is a fraction expressed as a proportion of 100.
6. A half is a ____________. Expressed as a ____________, it is 0.5.
7. 30 ____________ by 30 is 900. 900 ____________ by 30 is 30.
8. ____________ is the opposite of division, and addition is the opposite of ____________.
9. Multiplication is really doing ____________ again and again and again.
   ____________ is really doing subtraction again and again and again.
10. We say 'an ____________ of money' but 'a number of coins'.
11. Twenty-five ____________ fifteen ____________ ten.
12. To spell ____________ correctly, remember *age* is at its end.
13. We raised a ____________ of $3 000 for the children's charity.
14. Should we increase or ____________ the amount of liquid in the mixture?

Killer words

Study the words and tips and then write them without looking back.

enough	Remember: it rhymes with *stuff* but isn't spelt like it.	____________
answer	Use a spelling pronunciation: say *ans-WER*.	____________
either	Use a spelling pronunciation: say *EE-EYE-ther.*	____________
neither	Learn with *either*.	____________
exactly	It helps to pronounce it correctly.	____________

Use the **Killer words** in this paragraph.

That's ____________ time to get your ____________ down. I want each pair of students to show me ____________ what they wrote down. The answer could be ____________ in numbers or words. However, remember this is a maths competition. So ____________ of you should tell anyone else what you've written.

Looking at ... *sion* words

In Unit 4 (page 22), you learnt that most nouns ending in a ***shun*** sound are spelt ***tion***, e.g. *addi**tion***.

However, some ***shun*** nouns are spelt ***sion***, e.g. *exten**sion**;* ***sion*** is also the ending for most nouns ending in a ***zhun*** sound, e.g. *ver**sion***.

1 Write out these ***sion*** words and say them out loud. Write ***sh*** if the word has a shun sound and ***zh*** if the word has a ***zhun*** sound.

tension	dimension	confusion	erosion	division	occasion
extension	comprehension	conclusion	explosion	television	persuasion
suspension	excursion	decision	vision	revision	version

2 Which words from the ***sion*** list are synonyms for the words below?

a outing ______ b sight ______

c stress ______ d separation ______

e end ______ f understanding ______

g puzzlement ______ h size ______

3 Take notice of word patterns when you write out spelling lists.

a Which three words follow the same pattern as *vision?*

b Did you notice that many ***sion*** words are from verbs or adjectives ending in a ***d*** sound, e.g. *divi**d**e/divi**sion***, *conclu**d**e/conclu**sion***. What ***d*** verbs or adjectives do these words come from?

i tension ______ ii extension ______

iii suspension ______ iv comprehension ______

v decision ______ vi erosion ______

vii explosion ______ viii persuasion ______

4 Make up sentences using these ***sion*** word pairs.

excursion – television

confusion – comprehension

revision – division

____

____

conclusion – version

____

____

explosion – extension

____

____

5 Make up a short, fun poem about mathematics using ***sion*** words or other words from the unit. Here's mine.

Please no more revision ______________________________
of that horrible long division. ______________________________
I'm sure it's terrible for my vision. ______________________________
Can't I just watch television? ______________________________

Word scramble

Which words from the **Topic spelling list** are scrambled below?

1 DDNITOIA	______________	2 STARTINOCBUT	______________
3 TESTMIEA	______________	4 TRAPGEEECN	______________
5 NOTCARIF	______________	6 NOTPICTUMLILAI	______________
7 LADMICE	______________	8 NIVSIDIO	______________

Proofreading

Without looking back at any words from the lists in this unit, can you correct this student's spelling test? Tick the correct spellings, put a cross against the incorrect ones and write in the correct spelling. When you finish your corrections, look back and check that you were right.

avrage	______________	graph	______________	answer	______________
pluss	______________	multiplyed	______________	enought	______________
addition	______________	precentage	______________	ither	______________
devide	______________	ammount	______________	division	______________
minus	______________	quarter	______________	extention	______________
decrease	______________	equal	______________	totall	______________

Vocabulary power

If you know the meanings of common prefixes, you can work out what new words mean. Look at the chart of **Latin prefixes** below:

Prefix	Meaning	Example
multi-	many	multiply
sub-	under	subtract
super-	above	supermarket
auto-	self	automatic
pre-	before	preface
inter-	between, among	interval
ex-, e-	out of	exit
trans-	across	transfer

1 Write down what you think these words mean, using your knowledge of prefixes. Then look the words up in the dictionary to check if you were right. For example:
prejudice means judging someone or something before you know them.

a multilingual ______________________

b multitude ______________________

c interact ______________________

d autodestruct ______________________

e extract ______________________

2 Which words am I thinking of?

a a *multi-* word meaning *many cultures* ______________

b a *sub-* word meaning *a section of a city* ______________

c a *super-* word meaning *watch over* ______________

d an *auto-* word meaning *vehicle* ______________

e a *pre-* word meaning *guess the future* ______________

f an *inter-* word meaning *stop something* ______________

g an *ex-* word meaning *outside* ______________

h a *trans-* word meaning *change* ______________

Dictionary search

Look in your dictionary to find other words beginning with the prefixes above. Choose five that would be useful for you and jot down their meanings below.

____

____

Read and learn

Read this text about mathematical magic tricks, and try to work out the meanings of the words in **bold**.

Many magic tricks **exploit** the magical properties of numbers. Most of them require no skill. You simply have to follow the instructions and the tricks work by themselves. In other words, you don't need to use any **deception**. You do, however, need to do some mental arithmetic in many and concentrate hard in order to memorise numbers. Of course, you don't have to let the audience know you are just following a **straightforward** procedure. You must pretend you are using **mental telepathy** if you want to **convey** a sense of mystery and suspense. It will help if you don't say that you are doing a 'trick'. Instead, you should say you are doing an 'experiment' or 'test'. This is more likely to make your audience believe you are mind-reading. You can **reinforce** this impression with some dramatic movements and facial gestures.

Now circle the answer which best gives the meaning of each word as it is used in the text.

1	exploit	a	exercise	b	make use of	c	introduce
2	deception	a	hiding the truth	b	acting	c	mind-reading
3	straightforward	a	straight	b	simple	c	complicated
4	mental telepathy	a	mind-reading	b	telephone a friend	c	thinking
5	convey	a	show	b	learn	c	communicate
6	reinforce	a	make stronger	b	hide	c	decrease

Puzzle

Which words from the **Topic spelling list** are scrambled below?

SSOALLIUIUGIPDMNTTT ______________________________

Do you know this word?

An ***alternative*** (noun) is a choice. For example:

*You have two **alternatives**: you can get a lift with me now or you can walk home later.*

Your turn to write

Choose one of the following tasks. Do your writing on your own paper, but make sure you do a rough draft first. Revise and edit your work, and then write it out again.

1. How much do you like mathematics? You may love it or hate it. You might like some of the things you do in maths lessons, but dislike others. Write a paragraph or two to express your feelings about the subject. Try to use the words from the **Topic spelling list**.

OR

2. Do you know a magic maths trick? Write about how you do it. You could begin with a list of the things you need, e.g. coins, paper, etc.

☞Answers on page 153

13 Experimenting and building

Use this space to write out your topic words the first time. Use your own paper for extra practice.

Rewrite here those you had most trouble with.

Quick fun

How many colours can you make out of these letters? There are 11.

ITEPBLPELABLENOWNGOOLWACKRRREUUEEETEDYLLORGENVIPKINBRWH

Topic spelling list

timber
metal
build
experiment
cardboard
rubbish
material
collect
procedure
separate

piece
scissors
science
method
equipment
instructions
design
diagram
gently
carefully

Masterful memo

Use **mnemonics*** (memory tricks) to help you remember words. For example: you might remember the ***pie*** in ***pie***ce if you think of a ***pie***ce of ***pie***.

Write out the words from the **Topic spelling list** using any memory tricks you know.

* The *m* is silent.

Fill in the gaps

Fill in the gaps with words from the **Topic spelling list**. You might need to add ***s*** or ***ed***.

1. You can make the legs of the table with ____________ or ____________.
2. The teacher asked the children to bring in any old ____________ from home that could be recycled for the project.
3. We had to do a ____________ of what we planned to build before we started work.
4. What kind of ____________ is best to use: cotton or synthetic?
5. I don't want you to choose any ideas that need expensive ____________.
6. Follow the exact ____________ if you want the experiment to work.
7. Use a ____________ of ____________ or thick paper.
8. Which ____________ is best: using a razor or a pair of ____________?
9. You can ____________ your structure with any materials you like, even Lego.
10. Shake the container ____________, making sure you don't spill any liquid.
11. ____________ as many ice-cream containers as you can.
12. Push the wheel ____________ if it does not spin freely.
13. We left the mixture for half an hour so that the oil and water would ____________.
14. My favourite part of the week is Wednesday afternoon because we have ____________ club and do lots of interesting ____________.
15. The ____________ were written very clearly, but we still couldn't make our experiment work.

Killer words

Study the words and tips and then write them without looking back.

coloured	Remember the colour *red* and you'll get the end right.	____________
pattern	Think of *fatt**er***, *matt**er***, *patt**er*** to remember the ***er***.	____________
cloth	Means fabric, material or rag.	____________
clothes	Means what you wear (e.g. shirt).	____________
drawing	Just add ***ing*** to *draw*. You may hear an ***r*** sound (*draw-**r**-ing*), but it is not written.	____________

Can you use all the **Killer words** in one sentence?

____

____

Looking at … long e sound spelt *ie*

Most words with a **long e sound** are spelt with **e** (*th**e**se*), **ee** (*d**ee**p*) or **ea** (*cl**ea**n*). However, in some words the long **e** is spelt ***ie***, e.g. *p**ie**ce*.

Note: A few words use ***ei*** for the long **e** sound, e.g. *rec**ei**ve*, *rec**ei**pt*, *c**ei**ling*, ***ei**ther*, *n**ei**ther*, *w**ei**rd*.

1 Match the ***ie*** words below to their synonyms. Notice the patterns, e.g. *br**ie**f* and *th**ie**f*.

piece	fierce	priest	thief	believe
niece	field	chief	siege	belief
pier	shield	grief	tier	relief
pierce	shriek	brief	achieve	relieve

a row ________ **b** meadow ________ **c** cry out ________

d short ________ **e** sorrow ________ **f** jetty ________

g bit ________ **h** minister ________ **i** battle ________

j robber ________ **k** boss ________ **l** make better ________

m reach ________ **n** feeling of gladness ________

2 Which ***ie*** words from the list could go in these phrases?

a a protective ________ **b** ________ the heart

c a ________ of delight **d** overcome with ________

e what a ________ **f** fall to ________s

g ________ of police **h** catch a ________

i ________ a goal **j** hard to ________

k a ________ battle **l** a high ________

Looking at … *ic* and *al* adjectives

We often make **adjectives from nouns and verbs** by adding ***ic*** or ***al***, e.g. *science* → *scientif**ic***, *experiment* → *experiment**al***. Sometimes we need to double or change letters before adding the ending, e.g. *metal* → *meta**llic***, *office* → *offic**ial***.

Make adjectives from these nouns using ***ic*** or ***al***.

1 graph ________ **2** acid ________ **3** base ________

4 cube ________ **5** rhythm ________ **6** period ________

7 strategy ________ **8** dynamo ________ **9** volcano ________

10 history ________ **11** magnet ________ **12** essence ________

13 digit ________ **14** substance ________ **15** accident ________

16 idea ________ **17** practice ________ **18** metre ________

Proofreading

Can you correct the spelling mistakes in this student's report?

Durring the year, we had Sience Club meetings once a fornight on Wenesday afternoons. We did lots of intresting experments, althogh sometimes we didn't follow Mr Tran's instrushons carfully enuff, and things did not turn out quiet right. We used lots of sientific equipmen like microscopes, test tubes and beakers. However, mostly we used recyceld rubish from home and everyday matterials that we had in the classroom. Jackson's father supplied us with timber and mettal from his work, and the local supermarket let us have as many cardbord boxes as we wanted. My favourite day was when we constructed briddges using only newspaper and sticky tape and scisors. The funnyest day was when Jackie let out all the ants from the ant farm and they got into the staffroom.

Vocabulary power

An **idiom** is a group of words that does not mean exactly what it says. For example, I might say *I am all at sea.* However, I don't mean *I am in the middle of the ocean.*
I mean *I am having a lot of trouble understanding.*

You can often work out an idiom's meaning from the individual words, but not always.

1 Do you know the idioms below? They are about **learning and working**. Each of them means something similar to one of the general ideas on the right. Draw lines to link the idioms to the correct meaning.

see the light

know something backwards

work your guts out

know something inside out

be in over your head

work your fingers to the bone

get the hang of something

get the picture

be in the dark

move mountains

be out of your depth

know something like the back of your hand

know or understand something very well

not know or understand something at all

eventually understand something

put in a lot of effort

2. Choose one of the idioms above to use in each space below. You'll have to change some words, e.g. *your* to *my* or *his*.

a He's a great worker. He ______________________________ to get the playground finished in time for school to begin.

b At first I couldn't understand how to do it, but then I suddenly ______________________________.

c I just can't do maths. I am ______________________________ in that class.

d He's a taxi driver. He ______________ the streets of Brisbane ______________________________
______________________________.

Read and learn

Sometimes you can work out the meaning of a word by thinking of a related word, e.g. the word *search* helps you understand the meaning of *research*.

Read the instructions for the experiment below, taking special note of the words in **bold**.

Light a candle, let it burn for a few minutes and then blow it out. While it's still smoking, hold a lighted match in the smoke **plume**. Watch carefully and you'll see the flame shoot down the smoke column and **reignite** the candle!

This happens because there is unburnt wax in the candle's smoke (which gives it that **characteristic** candle smell). This **vaporised** wax is **ignited** by the flame from the match, and carries the flame down to **reignite** the wick.

It's quite an impressive trick. If the air is still, and the smoke **plume** is quite thick and rising straight up, you can **reignite** the wick from as far away as 7 centimetres! Maybe you can do even better.

From 'Light my Fire', *The Helix* No. 45, December 1995–January 1996. Reproduced with permission.

1. Look at the meanings of the words below. Each word is related to one of the words in **bold**.

plumage	bird feathers
ignition	an action or device which starts something burning
character	particular features of a person or thing
vapour	gas

Do you know this word?

A ***hypothesis*** (noun: plural ***hypotheses***) is an idea based on facts but not yet proved. For example:

Many scientific experiments aim to prove a ***hypothesis****.*

2. Now use the meanings and the clues in the text to choose the correct meanings of the words **a–e**.

a plume	**i** a thin stream of smoke	**ii** a cloud
b reignite	**i** melt	**ii** catch alight again
c characteristic	**i** pleasant	**ii** typical
d vaporized	**i** changed into gas form	**ii** liquid
e ignited	**i** started	**ii** set alight

Puzzle

1. Which words from the lists in the unit rhyme with the words below? Warning: the spellings give no clues at all—you have to say the words out loud.

   a filled

   b fizzes

   c appliance

   d roaring

2. Which words from the **Topic spelling list** or **Killer words** sections hide the words below? The first one has been done for you.

   a A type of **food**. — **pie**ce (pie)

   b Another word for **rug**.

   c Another word for **man**.

   d A measurement of **weight**.

   e Past tense of **meet**.

   f A kind of **bird**.

   g A **colour**.

   h A three-letter **snake**.

   i A type of **vehicle**.

   j A word meaning **uncooked**.

   k A word meaning **pace** or **speed**.

Your turn to write

Think about something you know how to make or do. For example: make a cubbyhouse, perform a simple science experiment or magic trick, make a campfire or bake a cake. Write instructions for someone else to show them exactly what to do and in what order.

You will need to plan your writing before you start to be sure you have got things in the right order. Use the space provided below. Remember to revise and edit your writing.

 ☞ Answers on pages 153–154

14 A healthy body

Quick fun

How many little words can you make from the phrase A HEALTHY BODY?
Give yourself 60 seconds. There are at least 25.

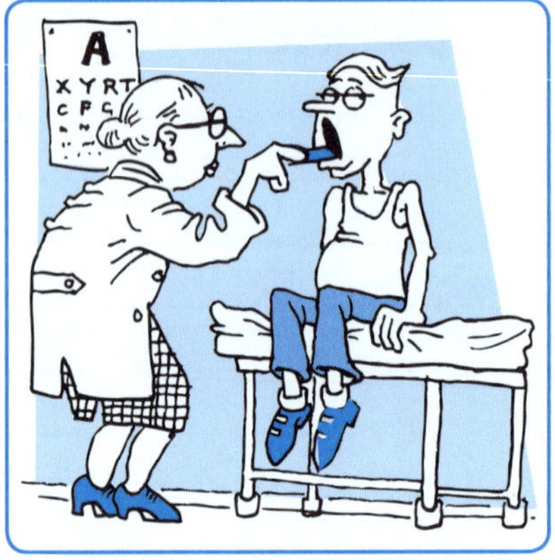

Topic spelling list

human	nervous
cells	circulation
genes	skeleton
genetic	balance
muscle	breath
muscular	breathe
senses	healthy
heart	physical
blood	energy
emotions	strength

Powerful pointer

Think of related words when spelling, e.g. ***heal*** helps you spell ***heal****th*; ***circ****le* helps you spell ***circ****ulate*.
Can you see any related word pairs in the list?

Write out the words from the **Topic spelling list** using the LOOK-SAY-COVER-WRITE-CHECK method.

Use this space to write out your topic words the first time. Use your own paper for extra practice.

Rewrite here those you had most trouble with.

Fill in the gaps

Fill in the gaps with words from the **Topic spelling list**. Add ***s*** or ***ed*** if needed.

1. There are about 208 bones and 639 ____________ in the ____________ body.
2. ____________ diseases can be inherited from your parents or other ancestors.
3. When you are frightened, you should try to stay calm and ____________ deeply.
4. The weight-lifter showed immense ____________ strength.
5. Our ears are very important for our sense of ____________.
6. Without your ____________, you would collapse like a heap of jelly.
7. You have about five litres of ____________ flowing around your body.
8. The body's system of ____________ is like a transport system taking oxygen and nutrients to where it is needed and taking waste away.
9. Electrical impulses run along the nerves in the body's ____________ system.
10. Your brain, which is the control centre of your body, has 10 million nerve ____________. It contains your memories, your thoughts and your ____________.
11. Athletes do constant training to develop their ____________ and flexibility.
12. About once every second, the walls of your ____________ contract and squeeze blood into strong tubes called arteries.
13. To stay ____________ and have lots of ____________, you should eat well. My grandmother says 'You are what you eat'.

Killer words

Study the words and tips and then write them without looking back.

body	Remember: *you have one body and bo**d**y has one* ***d***.	____________
activity	Say the syllables out loud so you won't miss one. Easy!	____________
exercise	Break into syllables: *EX-ER-CISE*. Remember the soft **c.**	____________
laughter	Chant the letters out loud with rhythm: *L-A-U-G-H-T-E-R*.	____________
stomach	Think of *stom**ach** **ach**e*: *ache* is hard too, but if you learn them together you might remember them.	____________

Use the **Killer words** in sentences. Try to use more than one word in each sentence.

____

____

____

____

Looking at … soft c words

Many words have a **c** for the **s** sound if it is followed by ***e***, ***i*** or ***y***, e.g. ***c****ells*, ***c****irculation*. This is called a **soft c**. A few words have **sc**, e.g. *mu**sc**le*.

1. Study the words below and write them out in alphabetical order. Remember: if the first letter is the same, look at the second letter. If the second letter is the same, look at the third, and so on. So ***ce****lls*, ***cir****cle*, ***circu****lation*.

city	census	fancy	notice	advance
citizen	citrus	recent	except	sentence
central	certain	recite	twice	civilisation
ceiling	cellar	service	excellent	fascinate

2. Two soft **c** words above are jumbled up in each letter string below, but the letters are in the right order. Can you work them out?

a RECECERTANTIN

b FCAITNYCY

c EXCECENTPRATL

d CIEXTICEZLLENENT

e TWFAICSCINEATE

f CECENSILIUSNG

g CITCERLLUSAR

h RESECNTIENTECE

i ADVCIVILANISCATEION

j SNOERTIVICECE

3. Look back at the **Topic spelling lists** from the last three units. Write down any soft **c** words you find (**c** or **sc** words).

Vocabulary power

Antonyms are **opposites**, for example *tall* and *short*. Sometimes there is more than one antonym for a word.

1 Draw lines between the **antonym** pairs **about the body** in the circle below. Use your dictionary if needed.

gradual dry upper alert strong clear
joined straight
robust soft rough
sudden graceful blunt separate delicate
straight final coarse
inferior moist relaxed lower fine
clumsy healthy initial
bent outer brittle
firm flexible stiff ill rigid supple calm
sharp curved
nervous gentle blurred
inner superior

2 We make many antonyms with the prefixes ***un-*** and ***in-***, e.g. ***un****healthy*, ***in****credible*. However, words beginning with ***p*** or ***m*** may make their opposites with the prefix ***im-***, e.g. ***im****polite*. We also make opposites by changing the suffix ***-ful*** to ***-less***, e.g. grace**ful** → grace**less**.

Can you add prefixes or change the suffixes to make opposites of these words?

a colourful	____________	**b** steady	____________
c mobile	____________	**d** sensitive	____________
e complete	____________	**f** dependent	____________
g flexible	____________	**h** frequent	____________
i practical	____________	**j** fearful	____________
k useful	____________	**l** mature	____________
m pure	____________	**n** active	____________
o attentive	____________	**p** ordinary	____________

3 Make up some **true** sentences about people you know using some of the antonym pairs in 1 and 2. Use your own paper.

Proofreading

Without looking back at any list words, can you correct this student's spelling test? Tick the correct spellings, put a cross against the incorrect ones and write in the correct spellings. When you finish your corrections, look back and check that you were right.

humman ______	circultion ______	laughter ______	exersise ______	skelton ______	stomack ______
genes ______	cells ______	twise ______	musell ______	breth ______	certain ______
heart ______	physical ______	exsept ______	blood ______	enegy ______	service ______
nervus ______	strenth ______	sentens ______	activity ______	body ______	living ______

Read and learn

Your own experiences can help you make sense of new words you meet when reading. I'm sure you've had the experiences explained here, so use them to work out the meanings of the words in **bold**.

Hiccoughs

Hiccoughs are one of the most annoying things in the world and one of the hardest things to get rid of. So what are hiccoughs and what causes them?

You probably know that the body has many reflexes. Reflexes are responses to some sort of **stimulation**. This means we have no control over them. The nerve connections in our bodies are programmed (a bit like a computer) and spring into action to make the same response every time there is that particular stimulation.

There are many reflexes that help us get solid and liquid food into our system and get rid of it (or any **foreign objects** like a pin or a broken tooth) as well. For example, there are a series of reflexes connected with swallowing food. When food goes down the wrong way, the **gagging** and choking that we all do are reflex actions to try to **expel** the food.

Sneezing and coughing are other normal reflexes in which a forceful blast of air is used to help the body **eject** material it does not want. Vomiting is a similar reflex, though much stronger. And hiccoughing is, in a way, an **ineffective** effort to vomit!

Hiccoughs might start because hot food has irritated some passage inside, or when gas in the stomach presses upward against the diaphragm (which separates the chest from the stomach). The diaphragm **contracts** and pulls air into the lungs. But the air can't get through and we feel a rather violent 'bump' at the moment the air is stopped. We say, if we can catch our breath, and usually with a tone of **desperation**: 'I've got the hiccoughs'.

Can you complete the definitions of the words below using the clues in the text above?

1	stimulation	Something which triggers a r __ a __ __ i o n.
2	foreign objects	Objects which don't b __ l __ __ __ .
3	gagging	Feeling like you are going to v __ __ __ __.
4	expel	Push something __ __ __.
5	eject	Same meaning as __ __ __ __.
6	ineffective	Not very u __ __ f u l.
7	contracts	T i __ __ __ e n s.
8	desperation	H __ p __ l e s s __ __ s s.

Did you know?

- Your body is about 70% water.
- Your brain is even more watery. It is about 80% water.
- An average person's skin would measure about 2 square metres if it was laid out flat, and weigh about $2\,^{1}/_{2}$ kilograms.

Puzzle

Can you complete this crossword using words from the unit? Some of the clues are a little cryptic, so you'll have to use all your brains.

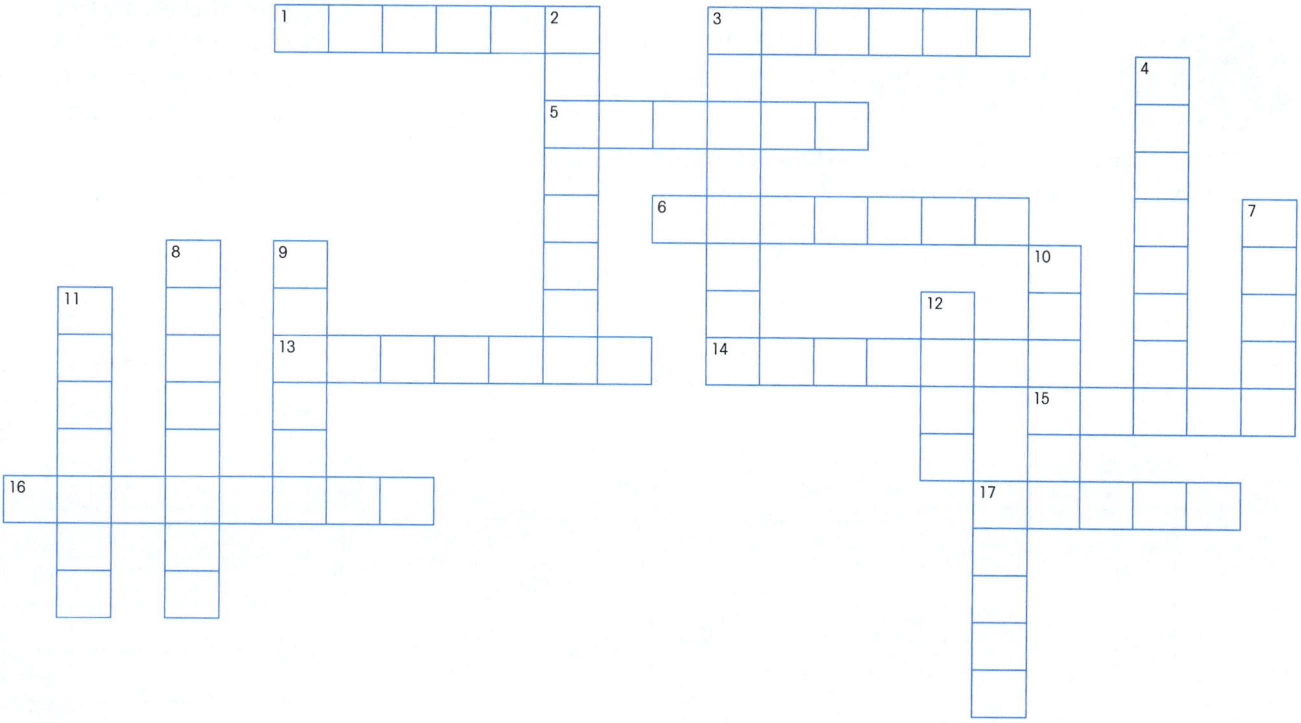

Across

1. Means the same as *opportunity.*
3. You have five of these.
5. A word meaning *but*.
6. An antonym of *ill.*
13. A member of the community (a town, city or country).
14. A synonym for *anxious.*
15. Sounds like *sells.*
16. People say ________________ is the best medicine.
17. This word is often used to mean *centre*.

Down

2. You might do this in a gym.
3. You might find this in a ghost story.
4. *Mental* is to *mind* as ______________ is to *body*.
7. A homophone for a kind of clothing.
8. An antonym of *weakness.*
9. Not long ago.
10. A homophone of a kind of seafood.
11. You might get an ache here.
12. No________, every__________, some____________, any_____________.
17. We are all only ______________.

Your turn to write

Create a poster to encourage people to take care of their bodies and keep healthy.

Give them some tips about what they can do and why. You might include something about their bones, their skin, their blood and circulation system, their muscles, their nervous system, or their digestive system.

You could include some interesting facts about the body using information in the unit or other facts you find out.

Do your poster on your own paper, but make sure you do a rough draft first. Add illustrations to make your poster attractive and interesting to read.

☞Answers on pages 154–155

15 Talking about time

Quick fun

Can you fill in the letters to spell the days of the week in this 'no clue' crossword? The vowels have been left to help you.

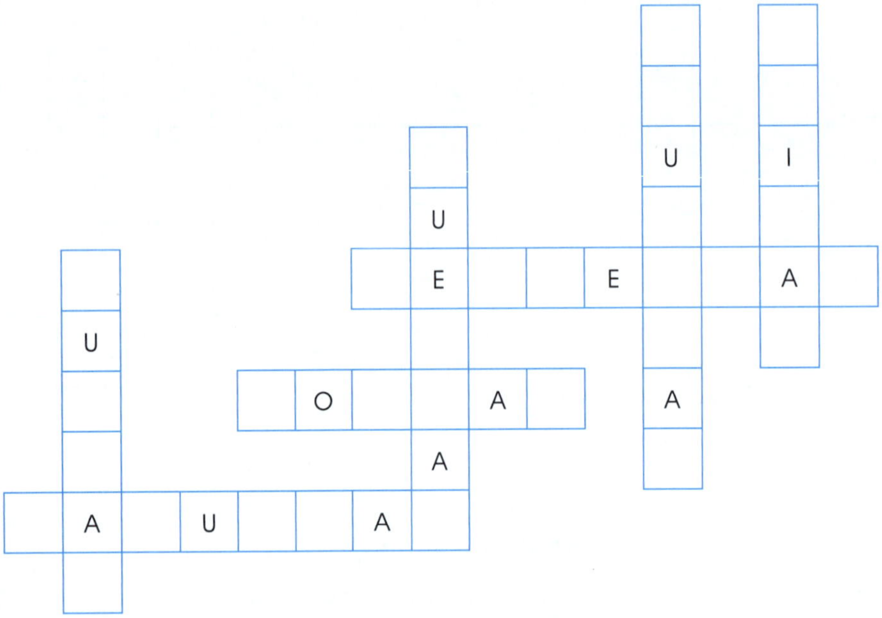

Use this space to write out your topic words the first time. Use your own paper for extra practice.

Rewrite here those you had most trouble with.

Topic spelling list

past
present
future
moment
yesterday
tomorrow
recently
meanwhile
schedule
season
fortnight
decade
monthly
afterwards
beforehand
nowadays
twenties
immediately
thousand
millennium

Timely tip

When you copy out words to learn, try to write the whole word in one go (or perhaps two). Don't just copy one or two letters and look back for the next ones. This will help you remember the spelling.

Write the words from the **Topic spelling list** using this strategy.

Fill in the gaps

Fill in the gaps with words from the **Topic spelling list**.

1. It is fun to try to predict the ______________, but mostly we get it wrong.
2. Does the next ______________ start in the year 3000 or 3001?
3. She is on the phone at the ______________, but she'll be free ______________.
4. We have a maths test every ______________ and a ______________ spelling test.
5. We went on an excursion to the zoo ______________ afternoon, and ______________ morning we'll go to the museum.
6. The swimming pool should be open all day Sunday, but it is a good idea to call ______________.
7. The swimmers had a strict training ______________ which left them with very little free time.
8. I was born in the last ______________ of the twentieth century.
9. I asked you to do the dishes ______________, not in half an hour.
10. Most people move out of home sometime in their ______________.
11. When spelling, don't confuse '______________' with *passed*. They sound the same.
12. People spend much less time walking and doing physical work ______________ than they did a______________ years ago.

Killer words

Study the words and tips and then write them without looking back.

beginning	There are three ***n***s to remember.	______________
often	***Ten*** times is of***ten***.	______________
listen	Learn *lis****ten*** with *of****ten*** and remember the ***ten***.	______________
hour	Think of the ***h****our* ***h****and* on the clock to remember the ***h***.	______________
our	You'll get this right if you remember the one above.	______________
minute	Use a spelling pronunciation: say *min-UTE*.	______________

Try to use all the **Killer words** in one sentence. Can you do it?

____

____

____

____

Looking at … ordinal numbers

Some **ordinal numbers** are easy to spell: they simply add ***th*** to the **cardinal number**, e.g. *seven* → *seven**th***. Others change a letter before adding ***th***, e.g. *sixt**y*** → *sixt**ieth*** or are different words altogether, e.g. *one* → *first*.

1. Look at the list of ordinal numbers below. Underline those that change a letter or are completely different words from the cardinal form.

first	fifth	ninth	thirteenth	seventeenth	thirtieth
second	sixth	tenth	fourteenth	eighteenth	ninetieth
third	seventh	eleventh	fifteenth	nineteenth	hundredth
fourth	eighth	twelfth	sixteenth	twentieth	thousandth

2. Which ordinal numbers are written backwards below?

a HTFLEWT ____________ b HTEITNEWT ____________

c DRIHT ____________ d HTNEETRIHT ____________

e HTDNASUOHT ____________ f TSRIF ____________

g HTFIF ____________ h HTHGIE ____________

i HTEITROF ____________ j HTRUOF ____________

3. Write three **true** sentences to answer the questions. Use at least one ordinal number in each answer.

a Which is the first birthday you remember and why?

b Which birthday celebration was the most fun and why?

c Which future birthday are you most looking forward to and why?

____

____

____

Looking at … contractions

You probably know that **contractions** are words like *he'll*, *don't* and *I've*, formed when **two or more words are shortened into one single word** (*he'll = he will; don't = do not; I've = I have*).

Contractions can be tricky to spell. You have to use an apostrophe to show where letters are missing, and you may have to change some letters.

Make sure you know all the contraction patterns below. Then follow the patterns to answer the questions.

I'm	you're	you'll	wasn't
she's (she is, she has)	they're	I'll	can't
who's	they've	he'd (he had, he would)	won't
it's	would've	you'd	shan't

1. Put the apostrophes where needed in these sentences.

   a Shell be turning one hundred next month. Were giving her a big party.
   b The children arent going to the celebration tomorrow. Theyre very disappointed.
   c We wont have our weekly test today. Ive changed it to next Monday.
   d If you studied harder, youd pass easily. Im sure you know that.
   e Weve told you a thousand times already, but you just havent listened.
   f Whos registered for tomorrow's program? Isnt everyone going?
   g He didnt know shed moved to the city.
   h Dont tell anyone youre coming. Itll be a surprise.

2. People sometimes have trouble with *it's* and *its*. Remember:
   it's means *it is* or *it has*. For example:
   It's (It is) raining.
   It's (It has) been raining all week.
   Its (without an apostrophe) means *belonging to it*. For example:
   I don't know who the dog belongs to. Its collar (the collar of *it*) *is missing.*

   Put *its* or *it's* into the following sentences.

   a The cat licked ________ plate clean.
   b I can't believe ________ not open.
   c The window won't open. ________ lock is broken.
   d Shall I open the dishwasher. ________ finished.
   e ________ time to go.
   f I can't tell you. ________ a secret.
   g You can't tell a book by ________ cover.
   h ________ a terrific party.

Proofreading

Can you correct the spelling errors in this student's writing? Remember to look for words from previous units as well as this one.

My great-grandparens grew up in the ferst few deccades of the 20th centry. Theyre both in their ninetys now, but they still tell me storys about what it was like all those yeers ago. Yestaday, when I went to see them, they told me about what they used to do for entertainment at night when they were yung. They said that theyd spend ours after dinner reading books or lissening to music on the gramophone—a kind of record player. Sometimes they even used to dance at home. On the weekends, they often went out to visit frends and occasionally they went to dances at the town hall. Afterwoods, they would walk around the town and meet up with other friends for an ice-cream or a cup of tea. Nowdays they still like to lissen to music, but they usualy wotch television like us. There allways saying that it was better in the old days.

Vocabulary power

1 Learning **synonyms** (words with similar meanings) is a good way to expand your vocabulary. Choose a word or phrase **about time** from the box to match its synonym below. Use your dictionary if you need to.

currently	simultaneously	previously	promptly	moment	eternal	final
frequently	subsequently	shortly	eventually	continuous	temporary	short

a soon ______________ **b** minute ______________

c uninterrupted ______________ **d** often ______________

e brief ______________ **f** immediately ______________

g impermanent ______________ **h** unending ______________

i last ______________ **j** after a time ______________

k beforehand ______________ **l** afterwards ______________

m at present ______________ **n** at the same time ______________

2 Now choose a word from the box in 1 above to use in these sentences.

a The ______________ noise from my brother's drumming gave my Dad a headache.

b The boys began the race ______________ but the smaller one finished first.

c Mrs Jones is ______________ teaching Year 5, but she usually teaches Year 6.

d The family ______________ travel overseas—at least four times a year.

e My sister has a ______________ job at the hospital, but it finishes in April.

f You have my ______________ gratitude for your great kindness.

g Answer ______________ when I speak to you.

h I'll be there ______________, but I have to eat lunch first.

Puzzle

Which three words from the **Topic spelling list** can you find in these letters?

STESRAPTUEPENUFRT

Do you know this word?

The adjective ***chronological*** means arranged in the order of time. For example:

*The teacher asked us to put the historical dates in **chronological** order.*

The prefix ***chron-*** means time. Do you know the meanings of these other ***chron*** words?

chron*icle*, ***chron****ic*

Try this brainteaser: I occur once in every minute, twice in every moment, but not once in a hundred thousand years. What am I? ______________________________

Read and learn

Reading a text about the past can be difficult because it is about experiences we can only imagine, and may contain words which describe things no longer used. Read the text below and answer the questions.

Message machines

Nowadays we communicate with people on the other side of the world with great ease. We can make a phone call, or send a text message or email. However, it was not always so easy.

Before any message-sending machines were invented, people sent signals using smoke, drums, fire bells and flashing mirrors. One of the first machines was called a semaphore. This had mechanical arms which could be pulled in different directions to make signs for different letters. Semaphore stations were usually on top of hills. People at one station took the message and then sent it on to the next station. The process was slow but faster than men could manage on horseback. Another kind of message machine was the shutter telegraph which worked by opening and closing shutters in different ways.

Then came the electric telegraph machine which transmitted electric currents. However, this only became practical as a message machine when Samuel Morse worked out a way to use it to send words. The sender tapped out different sets of dots and dashes for each letter, and at the other end, far away, the receiver decoded the dots and dashes into words.

The telephone was a major milestone. It worked by turning the sound of a voice into electric currents and then back into voice sounds at the other end of the line. In the beginning, however, you could not speak directly to the person you were calling. You had to ring the telephone exchange, where an operator connected you to the number you wanted. This changed with the invention of the automatic switchboard.

With the 20th century came the wireless—an extraordinary advance. For the first time, communication was possible across vast distances without any wires at all. Instead, radio waves carried the signals—and still do. Mobile phones are basically very sophisticated radios. They send radio waves to base stations, which then send them onto others—a bit like the semaphore stations of the past!

Now we have another important invention to help out: space satellites. These help to transmit radio, television and telephone signals across the planet and even the universe.

1 Draw a line to match the inventions (**a–d**) with the images.

a

b

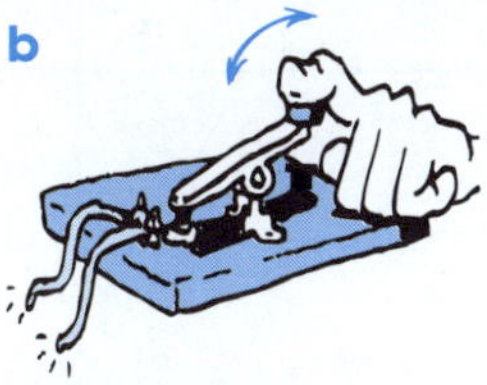

c

d

semaphore — shutter telegraph — morse code telegraph — radio transmission

2 Based on what you have read, do you think these statements are true (T) or false (F)? (Circle one.)

a Electric telegraphs transmitted the sound of voices. T / F

b The automatic switchboard saved time when telephoning. T / F

c The mobile phone is a kind of 'wireless'. T / F

d Space satellites take radio signals further than was possible before. T / F

3 What is a mobile phone base station compared to? ______________________________

Your turn to write

Write about a part of life that has changed over past decades or centuries, such as entertainment, housing, travel, clothes or photography. Include a few sentences about how you imagine this will change in the future.

☞ Answers on page 155

Review 3

Now let's see what you remember of the words you learnt in Units 11–15.

Step 1 Look at each group of words in the test to revise the spellings.

Step 2 Cover the five words up and test yourself (column 2). Try to do all five words in one go.

Step 3 Write your score out of 5 in the box. If you got any words wrong, go back and study them again.

Step 4 If possible, ask someone to test you on the words later—an hour or even a day later (column 3).

Test 1

Study	Test yourself	Test with another person
backwards towards movement mobile whirl	/5	/5
suddenly motionless velocity accelerate competition	/5	/5
won nearly rhythmic virtue thirsty	/5	/5
multiplication addition division divide decrease	/5	/5
percentage graph digit fraction decimal	/5	/5
enough answer either extension exactly	/5	/5
	Total score = out of 30	Total score = out of 30

Test 2

Study	Test yourself	Test with another person
neither comprehension excursion conclusion decision	/5	/5
explosion revision occasion persuasion version	/5	/5
metal separate build cardboard material	/5	/5
collect procedure piece scissors science	/5	/5
method equipment instructions design diagram	/5	/5
gently carefully pattern achieve drawing	/5	/5
	Total score = out of 30	Total score = out of 30

Test 3

Study	Test yourself	Test with another person
pierce brief tier clothes coloured	/5	/5
human cells genetic muscle senses	/5	/5
blood nervous circulation balance breathe	/5	/5
laughter stomach certain except gradually	/5	/5
excellent fascinate hurrying wander followed	/5	/5
physical strength body activity exercise	/5	/5
	Total score = out of 30	Total score = out of 30

Test 4

Study	Test yourself	Test with another person
immediately millennium beginning often minute	/5	/5
present future tomorrow recently schedule	/5	/5
fortnight decade monthly afterwards nowadays	/5	/5
third fifth eighth ninth twelfth	/5	/5
thirteenth twentieth twentieth thousandth they've would've	/5	/5
can't won't amount average multiplied	/5	/5
	Total score = out of 30	Total score = out of 30

Which word?

1. Can't you see ______________ snowing? (*its, it's*)
2. I'll tell you ______________ won in a minute. (*whose, who's*)
3. It took one whole ________________ to do my homework. (*hour, our*)
4. The show starts at half _________________ ten. (*passed, past*)
5. ______________ in big trouble now. (*Your, You're*)
6. ________________ in the back row of the hall. (*There, They're*)

How did you go? Did you do better than in the last review?

☞Answers on page 156

16 Money, money, money

Quick fun

1. How many little words can you make from MILLIONAIRE? There are at least 30.

2. Can you unscramble these places where you might go to spend your money?

   a ZPLAA ____________

   b LLAM ____________

   c CAREAD ____________

   d TENREC ____________

   e KARMET ____________

   f EQUARS ____________

Topic spelling list

bargain	unique
exchange	appliances
discount	catalogue
advertisement	budget
aisle	suitable
millionaire	receipt
quantity	purchases
quality	persuade
department	essentials
expensive	extravagant

Million-dollar strategy

Thinking of the base word will often help you spell a longer word, e.g. remember the ***ise*** in *adverti**se**ment* by thinking of the base word *adverti**se***.

Write out the words from the **Topic spelling list** using the LOOK-SAY-COVER-WRITE-CHECK method.

Word scramble

Which words from the **Topic spelling list** are scrambled below?

1. UUINQE ____________
2. UTALGOACE ____________
3. SESCAHRUP ____________
4. PENVISEEX ____________
5. LIATSSESNE ____________
6. AGRABIN ____________
7. LETUSIBA ____________
8. TENDRAVESTIEM ____________

Use this space to write out your topic words the first time. Use your own paper for extra practice.

Rewrite here those you had most trouble with.

Fill in the gaps

Fill in the gaps with words from the **Topic spelling list**. Change the ending of the words if needed.

1. My brother is saving up to travel overseas, so he is on a very strict ____________. He is only spending on ____________.
2. I love shopping with my dad. He spends hours playing with the electrical ____________ and I get to explore all the other shopping ____________.
3. Dad says I'll never be a ____________ if I keep spending all my pocket money.
4. It's a good idea to keep the ____________ when you buy things. It makes it easier to ____________ them or get a refund if they are not ____________.
5. My mother loves going to garage sales. She comes back very excited about her ____________, but my father says they are all just rubbish. She just can't ____________ him that they are all great ____________.
6. Finally we are getting a new television, so we looked through all the ____________ from the local ____________ stores to find the one we liked most.
7. The ____________ said that the special ____________ would last till Friday but when we went to the shop, everything was back to the usual price.
8. My sister takes hours to find her clothes. She's very fussy. She wants good ____________ but not at an expensive price. She also likes to find clothes that are ____________ so she won't see them on anyone else.
9. It's usually best to buy in large ____________ because you save some money.
10. Mum reckons she's only ____________ when she buys perfume.

Killer words

Study the words and tips and then write them without looking back.

money	Remember the ***one*** in *m**one**y*.	____________
buy	Think of *b**u**y* *b**u**tter* to remember the ***u***.	____________
bought	Learn with *brought*, *thought*, *fought*, *nought* and *ought*.	____________
paid	Remember: it's irregular—learn with *said*.	____________
necessary	Remember: one ***c**ollar* and two ***s**ocks* in *ne**c**e**ss**ary*.	____________

Try to use all the **Killer words** in one sentence. If you can't manage one sentence, make it two.

Looking at … *en*, *an*, *ain*, *in*, *ine*, *on* and *ern* words

Many words in English end in a sound like ***eh*** + ***n***. This ***eh*** sound is called a ***schwa***. Unfortunately, there are many different ways to spell this sound—as you can see in the table below. Because of this, it is always best to check your dictionary whenever you are not sure about this ending.

en	*an*	*ain*	*in*	*ine*	*on*	*ern*
broken	human	bargain	cabin	engine	bacon	modern
even	slogan	captain	napkin	masculine	demon	eastern
swollen	orphan	certain	dolphin	feminine	button	western
token	tartan	curtain	goblin	examine	crimson	southern
rotten	urban	mountain	javelin	medicine	dragon	northern
happen	woman	villain	bulletin	famine	lemon	govern

1 Which words from the table am I thinking of?

- **a** A purplish-reddish colour. ______________
- **b** Not old-fashioned at all. ______________
- **c** A purchase at a good price. ______________
- **d** A group of words to publicise a message, such as *slip, slap, slop*. ______________
- **e** Something you use instead of a coin, such as in parking meters. ______________
- **f** Bad, disgusting, off. ______________
- **g** The boss or chief of a team. ______________
- **h** The 'bad guy' in a play, film or book. ______________
- **i** A direction. ______________
- **j** To rule a country. ______________
- **k** A devil. ______________
- **l** A news report. ______________
- **m** The male gender. ______________

2 Now see if you can get these words. They are not in the lists above, but follow one of the patterns.

- **a** A lamp. L ___ ___ ___ E R N
- **b** Part of a plant. P ___ ___ ___ E N
- **c** A sharp claw on a bird. T ___ ___ O N
- **d** A kind of headgear. T ___ ___ ___ A N
- **e** A bit like a goblin. G ___ ___ ___ L I N
- **f** Decide. D ___ ___ ___ ___ ___ I N E
- **g** Stripes are an example. ___ ___ ___ ___ E R N
- **h** Something you throw. ___ ___ ___ ___ ___ I N

Vocabulary power

If you know the meaning of common word roots, it can help you work out the meanings of new words. For example: the **Latin word root ped** means *foot*: think of *centi**ped**e* and *milli**ped**e*. Look at these common word roots:

dict = *tell*, e.g. ***dict**ation*
ject = *throw*, e.g. *ob**ject***
termin = *end*, e.g. *de**termin**e*
pend = *hang*, e.g. *sus**pend***
rupt = *break*, e.g. *e**rupt***

1 Do you know these words from the above root words?

a A ***ped*** word meaning *person walking.* — PED _ _ _ _ _ _ _
b A ***dict*** word meaning *say something against, deny.* — C _ _ _ _ _ DICT
c A ***pend*** word meaning the same as *rely.* — _ _ PEND
d A ***ject*** word meaning *refuse.* — _ _ JECT
e A ***rupt*** word meaning *to break into a conversation.* — _ _ _ _ _ RUPT
f A ***termin*** word meaning *to end.* — TERMIN _ _ _

2 Now try to work out these words. Use your dictionary if needed.

a What kind of ruler is a *dictator*? ____________________
b What kind of jewellery is a *pendant*? ____________________
c What does *eject* mean? ____________________
d What does *corrupt* mean? ____________________
e Why is an airport, bus or train station sometimes called a *terminal*? ____________________
f What kind of body treatment is a *pedicure*? ____________________

3 Can you think of any other words from the roots above? ____________________

____

4 We have already looked at some **idioms** in Unit 13, but here we'll look at some others related to **money**. Always try to use the context to work out the meanings of any new idioms you see or hear. Underline the correct meaning of the idioms in **bold** in these sentences.

a John was really hurt by his brother's actions and said he would **pay him back**.
- i pay him some money to please him
- ii ignore him
- iii give him the same treatment later

b We told the sales assistant we did not want help. We were **window shopping**.
- i looking for windows
- ii looking not buying
- iii only shopping for things in the window

c My sister just got a part-time job so she's **spending money like water.**
- i spending a little
- ii spending a lot
- iii spending money on important things

d Mr Jones **has money to burn** and always wants to pay for everyone else.
- i has more than enough money
- ii has enough money
- iii burns his money for fun

e I wanted to get my jeans in City Central, but Mum said we'd **pay through the nose** there.
- **i** pay more than you should
- **ii** only find expensive things
- **iii** be cheated by the shopkeepers

f You had better clean up that mess now or **there'll be hell to pay**.
- **i** you'll have to pay for the damage
- **ii** you'll be in trouble
- **iii** you'll be paying for a long time

Do you know these words?

These two words are opposites.

A ***spendthrift*** loves spending money.

A ***tightwad*** hates spending money.

Read and learn....

Some words in the English language come from **people's names.** The word *scrooge* mean something even worse than *tightwad* (see box). Read this description of the original Scrooge, from the novel *A Christmas Carol* by Charles Dickens, and you'll understand why.

Oh! But he was a tight-fisted hand at the grindstone, Scrooge! A squeezing, wrenching, grasping, scraping, clutching, covetous old sinner! Hard and sharp as flint, from which no steel had ever struck out generous fire; secret, and self-contained, and solitary as an oyster. The cold within him froze his old features, nipped his pointed nose, shrivelled his cheek, stiffened his gait; made his eyes red, his thin lips blue; and spoke out shrewdly in his grating voice. A frosty rime was on his head, and on his eyebrows, and his wiry chin. He carried his own low temperature always about with him; he iced his office in the dog-days; and didn't thaw it one degree at Christmas.

There are some terrific words in this extract to describe Scrooge.

1. What do you think 'tight-fisted' means? ______________________

2. Write down the five ***ing*** words in the second line used to describe Scrooge's behaviour with money. Do they help you create a picture of Scrooge in your mind? ______________________

   ____

3. Look up 'covetous' in your dictionary and write down the meaning. ______________________

   ____

4. Is Dickens describing a picture of the cold temperature?
   - **a** inside Scrooge?
   - **b** outside in the air?
   - **c** both inside and outside?

5. Why does Dickens say Scrooge is 'solitary as an oyster'?
   - **a** Because he's hard to find.
   - **b** Because he wants to be alone.
   - **c** Because he's hard to talk to.

6. Do you understand now why it would be very insulting to call someone a *scrooge*? ______________________

   ____

Proofreading

Can you fix the spelling mistakes in this writing?

If you want to be a milionare, you should start thinking about saving muny right now. Try to resist those wonderful little bargans at the markits. Avoid strolling up and down the isles of deparment stores just for fun. Learn to resist those fantastic advertisments that try to perswaid you that a particular peace of clothing is necesary to avoid a life of misery! Most people who end up rich are very carful with there mony. They think about every cent they spend, examin every reseept and check every bit of change they are given. They never look through cataloges just to fill time—they might be tempted to by something! Most of them began their saving habits when they were small children—putting aside one dollar when they were given to, asking their pairents if they could keep the five cent peaces they didn't want. So don't think that these people are uneek in any way. They are just like you. They just take care of their munny.

Puzzle

Can you find 20 words from the **Topic spelling list** and **Killer words** in the wordsearch puzzle below? One long word goes diagonally.

D	P	Q	D	I	S	C	O	U	N	T	D	Y	V	E
E	U	U	B	O	U	G	H	T	N	D	D	T	S	S
R	R	A	P	E	R	S	U	A	D	E	H	Q	U	S
A	C	L	A	Z	S	O	G	T	Y	H	G	U	I	E
Y	H	I	N	E	Y	A	R	B	U	Y	B	A	T	N
U	A	T	Q	I	V	P	H	M	A	B	A	N	A	T
N	S	Y	P	A	I	D	B	C	B	R	R	T	B	I
I	E	A	R	U	E	Z	U	Z	R	W	G	I	L	A
Q	S	T	P	K	O	U	D	S	D	U	A	T	E	L
U	X	Q	V	A	R	T	G	A	F	A	I	Y	I	S
E	X	C	H	A	N	G	E	Z	L	R	N	O	G	N
S	R	A	D	V	E	R	T	I	S	E	M	E	N	T
Z	M	O	N	E	Y	L	R	E	C	E	I	P	T	A
A	I	S	L	E	T	N	E	C	E	S	S	A	R	Y

Your turn to write

Design and write an advertisement. It might be for a whole shop, for a sale or special, or for a particular item. Try to use some words from the unit. Remember that your aim is to attract and persuade people to come to your shop and buy your product, so use language which will help you achieve this purpose. You want to get the money out of the pockets of even those people who want to be millionaires!

You might want to look through a newspaper to find a few examples before you start. Use your own paper.

☞ Answers on page 156

17 Saving our planet

Quick fun

I am sure you know the name of our planet, but do you know the names of all the planets? Here are some clues. After you get all the names, number them from **1** to **8*** (**1** for the planet closest to the Sun).

- **a** Contains something we hear with.
- **b** You'll find this in a thermometer.
- **c** Ends with a pronoun.
- **d** Contains a word for a hole.
- **e** The name of a chocolate bar.
- **f** Ends with a song.
- **g** Contains a word for a vase.
- **h** Ends with the same pronoun as the other planet.

* There are now only eight planets. Do you know the name of the one which is no longer considered a planet?

Topic spelling list

waste	ozone layer
climate	destroy
pollution	awareness
chemical	environment
toxic	compost
plastic	community
resources	reduce
conserve	recycle
garbage	behaviour
protection	responsibility

Stratospheric strategy

Breaking longer words into syllables helps you hear all the sounds, e.g. *EN-VIR-ON-MENT*.

Write out the words from the **Topic spelling list** using the LOOK-SAY-COVER-WRITE-CHECK method.

Use this space to write out your topic words the first time. Use your own paper for extra practice.

Rewrite here those you had most trouble with.

Fill in the gaps

Fill in the gaps with words from the **Topic spelling list**. Change the endings if needed.

1. Australians throw away 900 000 000 ________ food containers each year.
2. There is a growing ________ in our ________ of the need to take care of our ________.
3. More than 75% of domestic rubbish could be ________, but only about 10% is.
4. All Australians are being educated not to ________ water. However, it is very difficult to change people's ________.
5. Air ________ occurs when air contains too many gases, dust, fumes or odours for humans and animals to live safely and comfortably.
6. Each person in Australia produces more than 13 kilograms of ________ per week.
7. ________ sometimes get into our waterways and affect water quality. They can be ________ for fish and animals as well as for humans.
8. There are many good ideas to ________, reuse and recycle paper, glass and cans.
9. Keeping a ________ bin is one good way to cut down on household garbage.
10. The oil leak ________ the surrounding forests and lakes.
11. Many environmentalists work hard for the ________ of endangered species.
12. The ________ blocks out harmful ultra-violet radiation which causes sunburn.
13. ________ change is a major concern at the moment, with temperatures rising by small amounts each year.
14. We can't just keep using up all our planet's ________. We have a ________ to ________ them for the next generations.

Killer words

Study the words and tips and then write them without looking back.

hole	Remember: *there's a **h**ole in my **h**at.*	________
whole	Remember: *a **wh**ole **wh**eel.*	________
choice	Learn with *voice*.	________
amongst	Chant out loud and remember the **o**.	________
neighbour	A difficult one! Use every strategy you know.	________

Use the **Killer words** in the spaces below.

The ________ talked ________ themselves about strategies to improve their local environment. Almost the ________ street was there. One man suggested digging a huge ________ in the bushland nearby and starting a communal compost pit. Another man said that nobody should be forced to change their habits—they should have a ________.

Looking at … irregular verbs

There are many **irregular verbs** in English and these can be tricky to spell, e.g. *choose, chose, chosen.*

*Can we **choose** our partners now?* (present tense)

*I **chose** my partner for the project last week.* (past tense)

*Have you **chosen** your partner yet?* (past participle)

Look at the irregular verbs below. Do you notice any patterns?

Present	Past	Past participle (e.g. *I have* …)	Present	Past	Past participle (e.g. *I have* …)
break	broke	broken	hide	hid	hidden
shake	shook	shaken	ride	rode	ridden
buy	bought	bought	leave	left	left
fly	flew	flown	mean	meant	meant
blow	blew	blown	say	said	said
know	knew	known	catch	caught	caught
draw	drew	drawn	show	showed	shown
drive	drove	driven	swim	swam	swum
eat	ate	eaten	wear	wore	worn
forgot	forgot	forgotten	hear	heard	heard

1 Use a verb from the list in these short sentences.

- **a** I ______________ the train at Central.
- **b** The small girl had ______________ her bike for three hours.
- **c** I've ______________ you how to make it many times.
- **d** Have you ______________ your new shirt yet?
- **e** All the test papers have ______________ away. Hooray!
- **f** You ______________ me all right, so don't pretend you didn't.
- **g** His whole body ______________ and his face was pale.
- **h** Have you ______________ any milk?
- **i** They ________ quickly to be in time for the competition.
- **j** My little sister ______________ all over the newly painted walls.

2 Use the patterns of any similar verbs in the lists to complete the table.

Present	Past	Past participle	Present	Past	Past participle
pay			tear		
wake			think		
teach			write		
sing			sleep		

Vocabulary power

Many English words contain Greek roots, prefixes or suffixes. For example: ***geo***, which means *earth*, is found in ***geo****logy*, ***geo****graphy* and ***geo****metry*; ***astro***, meaning *star*, is found in ***astro****logy* and ***astro****nomy*.

You can build up your knowledge of these **Greek word roots** by taking notice of similarities between words. You can then apply this knowledge to work out the meaning of new words.

1 Look at these word sets and then try to work out the meaning of each common Greek word root. It does not have to be exactly right—just a general meaning.

- a **anti**dote, **anti**biotic, **anti**septic *anti?* ______
- b **bio**logy, **bio**graphy, **bio**nic *bio?* ______
- c auto**graph**, para***graph***, **graph**ic *graph?* ______
- d **mono**rail, **mono**syllable, **mono**logue *mono?* ______
- e **micro**scope, **micro**phone, **micro**wave *micro?* ______
- f **syn**thetic, **syn**onym, **syn**chronise *syn?* ______
- g **therm**al, **therm**ometer, **therm**os flask *therm?* ______
- h **metr**ic, centi**metre**, dia**meter** *metre/ meter?* ______

2 Now work out what these words mean. You might know the meaning of some words. If so, think again about them with your new understanding of the Greek word-part. Use your dictionary to check the exact meaning.

a anticlimax	b micrometer	c monochrome
d monopoly	e monotonous	f synagogue

Proofreading

How did this student go in his unit spelling test? Tick the correct words and write any corrections. Did you get 100%?

garbig	______	destroid	______	showen	______
chemical	______	waiste	______	ment	______
plastic	______	enviroment	______	cawt	______
toksic	______	climate	______	worn	______
resorces	______	compost	______	pollution	______
conserve	______	community	______	choise	______
protection	______	reduse	______	amungst	______
ozone layer	______	recycleing	______	neighbour	______

Read and learn

Read this information from an environmental poster and think about the meanings of the words in **bold.**

A Gutful of Plastic

Floating rubbish, such as plastic, can be easily swallowed, and since it cannot be **digested** or **passed**, it stays in the whale. Plastic in the gut can prevent the animal from digesting its food and so may lead to starvation and death. This is because whales feed by swallowing large amounts of water, and use **baleen**, the fringe along the tops of their mouths, to **sieve** out small fish and other food.

In August 2000, an eight-metre Bryde's whale became **stranded** close to Central Cairns in north Queensland. It died soon after. An **autopsy** found that the whale's stomach was tightly packed with plastic—almost six square metres of it! The whale had swallowed supermarket bags, food packaging, three large sheets of plastic two metres long and **fragments** of garbage bags.

Please be careful with your rubbish. A plastic bag dropped in the street washes into **stormwater drains** which empty directly into the ocean. If you see plastic of any kind on the ground, don't let it become whale food. Pick it up!

1 Now choose the answer closest in meaning to the words **a–h**. Sometimes words have more than one meaning depending on the context. If you think both answers below are correct, choose the answer closest to the meaning as it is used in the text.

a digested	**i** swallowed into the body	**ii** processed in the body
b passed	**i** went by or moved past	**ii** pushed out of the body
c baleen	**i** part of the whale's mouth	**ii** part of the whale's stomach
d sieve	**i** chew up into small bits	**ii** separate small things from big
e stranded	**i** stuck on or near the shore	**ii** left alone, abandoned
f autopsy	**i** a team of scientists	**ii** an examination of the cause of death
g fragments	**i** packets	**ii** bits and pieces
h stormwater drains	**i** drains for stormy weather	**ii** drains taking rain and other water to the sea

2 *A Gutful of Plastic* is a clever title. Like many poster headings and newspaper headlines, it has a double meaning. One meaning is that the whale's gut gets filled with plastic. Can you identify its other meaning?

a enough, sufficient

b more than enough; too much

c not enough; needing more

3 A word in **1** above has a Greek prefix meaning *self*. It literally means *seeing with one's own eyes*.

Which word is it? ______________________

Do you know this word?

The noun ***ecology*** is a branch of biology. It is the study of how living things relate to their environment. It is another word with Greek origins: **eco** means *house* and ***ology*** means *science or study*.

Word scramble

Which words from the **Topic spelling list** are scrambled below?

1. GRABEAG ____________________
2. CUDEER ____________________
3. CALMIHEC ____________________
4. IRVENTMENON ____________________
5. TOTONCIPRE ____________________
6. YOSTDER ____________________
7. LEYERCC ____________________
8. STAPLIC ____________________

Puzzle

Can you complete this clueless crossword using words from the unit? Remember that some words might be from the **Killer words** and **Looking at …** sections.

Your turn to write

Design a poster to make people more aware of what they can do to protect and save our planet. You could choose a particular area: plastic bags, saving water, cars, air pollution, saving energy or recycling. Or you could keep your poster general and mention the main areas we need to focus on.

Try to use words from the unit. You could also use some of the environmental information in the unit. Use your own paper. Be sure to revise and edit your writing.

☞ Answers on pages 156–157

18 Different cultures

Quick fun

Can you unscramble these nationalities from places around the world?

1. GENSHIL _ _ _ ☐ _ _ _
2. QIIRA _ _ ☐ _ _
3. DONINIANES _ _ _ _ ☐ _ _ _ _ _
4. NAMGER ☐ _ _ _ _ _
5. UESEPORTUG _ _ _ _ ☐ _ _ _ _ _
6. SSURIAN _ _ _ _ _ ☐ _
7. IANETYPG _ ☐ _ _ _ _ _ _
8. KEGRE _ _ _ ☐ _
9. SEINECH _ _ _ _ _ ☐ _

Then write the letters from the boxes to make a word from the list that spells something they all use: ☐ ☐ ☐ ☐ ☐ ☐ ☐ ☐ ☐

Topic spelling list

culture	respect
cultural	attitude
social	belief
society	acceptance
traditional	prejudice
modern	difference
customs	gesture
language	fascinating
familiar	value
foreign	behaviour

Helpful hint

Remember to try out different ways of spelling words when in doubt. Often you will recognise which one looks right, e.g. ~~moden~~, ~~modden~~, ~~moddern~~, *modern*.

Learn the words from the **Topic spelling list** using the LOOK-SAY-COVER-WRITE-CHECK method.

Use this space to write out your topic words the first time. Use your own paper for extra practice.

Rewrite here those you had most trouble with.

Fill in the gaps

Fill in the gaps with words from the **Topic spelling list**. Add **s** to words if needed.

1. Many Chinese living outside China still celebrate Chinese New Year in the ________________ way.
2. What are the main ________________ between your country's culture and mine?
3. Science and technology has brought many changes to our ________________ in the past few decades.
4. Good ________________ and hard work is expected at this school.
5. It is easy to misunderstand the way people behave if we are not ________________ with their way of life. This can lead to ________________ and intolerance.
6. It is always ________________ to learn about the different ________________ of other cultures.
7. Travelling to ________________ lands makes us more aware of other ________________.
8. When we use ________________ and facial expressions to convey meanings, it is called body ________________. For example, we nod to show we agree with something.
9. Most individuals belong to many different ________________ groups: family, friends, neighbours, sports groups, church groups, and so on.
10. The ________________ and ________________ of the two cultures were very similar.
11. Most Asian countries have a very respectful ________________ towards their elders.
12. The school believed that ________________ of all cultures was very important. They expected everyone to ________________ each other at all times.

Killer words

Study the words and tips and then write them without looking back.

accept	The word *accept* means *take*; it *takes* two **c**s.	________________
except	The word *except* means *but*; learn it with *exciting*.	________________
recognise	Break it into syllables and you'll remember the ***g***.	________________
allowed	Remember: it is the past tense of *allow*. Just add ***ed***.	________________
aloud	Remember: it means *out loud*, so *aLOUD*.	________________

Use all the **Killer words** in sentences. Try to use two or three in the same sentence.

____

____

____

Looking at … words with the prefixes ex- and exc-

There are many words beginning with the **prefix ex**- in the English language, e.g. ***ex****tra*. It is a Latin prefix meaning *out of* or *from*, but it is often difficult to see this meaning in **ex** words.

exile	execute	expect	extinct	exhibit	exist
exam	example	expel	extract	exotic	exit
exercise	exhale	expensive	extreme	expert	exhausted

There are a few words beginning with the **prefix exc-** which are tricky because you can't hear the **c** clearly, e.g. ***exc****ept*. Pay special attention to these words.

excel	excellent	excite	exceed	exception	excess	excuse

1. Look up any **ex** words in the list above that you do not know the meaning of. Jot down their meanings below.

2. Use the clues below to fill in the boxes with **ex** words from the list above.

a	E	X	The way out.
b	E	X	Sent to another country.
c	E	X	Strange, unusual.
d	E	X	Show, display.
e	E	X	Activity, training.
f	E	X	Fatigued, tired.
g	E	X	The different one.
h	E	X	Of high quality.
i	E	X	Instance, pattern.
j	E	X	Go beyond.
k	E	X	Throw out.
l	E	X	Test.

3. Choose five **ex** words to use in your own sentences.

Proofreading

Can you correct the mistakes in this writing?

When you travel to a foren land, it is a good idea to become familar with the face, hand and body gesturs used by peeple in that regen to communicate meaning. This is called body langguage. For example, Inglish-speaking culshures show agrement by nodding their heds. They show disagrement by shaking their heds from side to side. It can be very serprising to see that there are diffrenses in the way other peple use body language. In some culshures, for example, the Inglish gesture for *no* meens *yes*.

Body langguage also includes how much we touch each other and how close we stand to each other. There are sometimes gender or age diffrenses, but usually there are unwritten rules in every sosyety about these matters. South Americans, for egsample, touch each other during conversashens much more than the French. The British hardly touch at all. This behavour can cause serious communicashun problems.

Vocabulary power

We looked at **idioms** in Units 13 and 16. Remember: an idiom is a group of words that doesn't mean exactly what it says. Instead it is a kind of metaphor, where you have to use your imagination to work out the meaning.

1. Can you guess the meanings of the idioms **about communication** on the left? Draw lines from each to one of the meanings on the right.

eat your words	tell you what you should say and think
get hold of the wrong end of the stick	say something very clearly
get your wires crossed	not be able to be heard because people are talking too much
be on the same wavelength	not be able to think of anything to say
speak with forked tongue	misunderstand each other
say it in words of one syllable	accept your opinion was wrong
can't get a word in edgeways	misunderstand what someone is saying
be stuck/lost for words	say exactly what someone else was going to say
have a word in your ear	understand each other well
put words in your mouth	tell lies
take words out of your mouth	say something secretly so that others don't hear

2. Look at the pictures above of the first three idioms listed. Do a quick drawing to illustrate one of the other idioms. Use your own paper.

Read and learn

When you research information for school assignments, you often have to deal with information written for people who are older than you. So you have to work out meanings of new words as you read.

Read this information text about culture, paying particular attention to the words in **bold**. Then choose which of the meanings below is correct.

What does 'culture' mean exactly? Many of us think of 'culture' as being to do with art galleries, museums, singing and dancing, orchestras, books and films, and refer to someone who spends a lot of time enjoying these things as 'cultured'.

However, to **sociologists,** culture is everything that a particular group of human beings has been **socialised** to do, think, use and make. It may include **material** things—artworks, clothing, tools, buildings and weapons. It also includes **intangible**, non-material things such as values, beliefs, customs, attitudes, knowledge and language. 'Culture' is also used to refer to a group of people who share this way of thinking and behaving—so for example, Hindu culture, Arabic culture, Fijian culture, Western culture.

Some examples might help to explain. Take kissing. Kissing is very much a cultural practice and rules and attitudes vary across the globe. The French and Italian kiss on greeting at least twice on each cheek, and very often three times, while English speakers generally only kiss once. Arabic and Russian men think nothing of greeting each other with a kiss, but men in English-speaking cultures would not dream of it. In Japan and some other Asian countries, kissing in public is generally regarded as unhygienic and **offensive**.

Shopping is another simple example. Travellers are sometimes **perplexed** to find that their usual shopping practices don't work out. In Australia, in general, a shopper is told the price of an item and the money is handed over—no argument. However, in many countries in Asia and the Middle East, shopkeepers would be insulted by this behaviour because shoppers are expected to **haggle** over prices.

Of course cultures change over time. They are influenced by **intercultural** contact and communication. We can even see this with kissing. Nowadays it seems that many English-speakers have adopted the European kissing style, perhaps influenced by French and Italian films. Kissing has become more **commonplace** in Asian countries, especially amongst younger people. And while kissing has not yet become a common public greeting amongst English speaking men, hugging is certainly **on the rise**—especially on the football field.

1. sociologists — **a** social people — **b** people who study social behaviour
2. socialised — **a** taught by their society — **b** taught social manners
3. material — **a** cloth, fabric — **b** real, observable
4. intangible — **a** hidden, hard to identify — **b** valuable
5. offensive — **a** insulting — **b** unclean
6. perplexed — **a** amused — **b** puzzled
7. haggle — **a** ask politely about — **b** argue
8. intercultural — **a** between cultures — **b** outside cultures
9. commonplace — **a** popular — **b** frequent
10. on the rise — **a** increasing — **b** seen

Do you know this word?

The adjective ***cosmopolitan*** means belonging to all parts of the world.
For example:
Fiona has very ***cosmopolitan*** *tastes in food since she got back from overseas.*

Puzzle

Which word from the **Topic spelling list** am I thinking of?

1. Rhymes with a ***v***-word meaning *bird of prey.* __________ (7 letters)
2. Contains an ***r***-word meaning *rule.* __________ (7 letters)
3. Ends with a little word meaning *about.* __________ (7 letters)
4. Starts with a little word meaning *about.* __________ (7 letters)
5. Ends with an ***l***-word meaning *fibber.* __________ (8 letters)
6. Ends with an ***a***-word about time. __________ (8 letters)
7. Has the pronoun ***us*** in the middle. __________ (7 letters)
8. Contains a ***lie***. __________ (6 letters)
9. Contains an ***m***-word meaning *method.* __________ (6 letters)
10. Contains a ***tan***. __________ (10 letters)
11. Ends with something you use in a boardgame. __________ (9 letters)
12. Rhymes with *saviour.* __________ (9 letters)

Your turn to write

Think about a culture you know well. It might be your own culture or that of a family member or friend. Choose one of the following tasks. Remember to do a rough draft first, and to revise and edit your writing.

1. Write about:

   - an important tradition (or traditions)
   - religious or spiritual beliefs
   - attitudes to family, e.g. children, the elderly
   - a festival or celebration
   - important values
   - roles of women and men

OR

2. Write about one or two of these areas of communication and body language in that culture. You might give examples and compare behaviour, e.g. between young and old, women and men, etc.

   How do people greet each other? e.g. do they kiss, hug, bow?
   Do people give complements? e.g. about food, house, clothing?
   How much do people touch each other when in conversation?
   What do they talk about? Are there some topics you cannot talk about?
   What are some commonly used gestures? e.g. to show agreement or disagreement, surprise, annoyance or unhappiness?
   What are the most important things to do to be polite?

☞ Answers on pages 157–158

19 The world of art

Quick fun

Do you know these famous artists? Fill in the missing letters. Ask a parent or friend for help if you need to.

1. P _ C _ S S _
2. M _ _ H E L _ _ _ E L O
3. L _ O _ A _ D _ D _ V _ _ C _
4. R _ _ B R _ _ D T
5. V _ N G _ G H

Topic spelling list

artistic	colourful
realistic	cartoon
gallery	exhibition
sculpture	create
illustration	masterpiece
skill	abstract
skilful	technique
graffiti	perspective
drawing	sketch
mural	portrait

Crafty tip

When in doubt about a word, write out the parts you are sure of and leave a blank for the part you don't know, e.g. *g a l l _ r y*. Then try different possibilities and decide which one looks better, e.g. ~~*gallary*~~, *gallery*.

Learn the words from the **Topic spelling list** using any strategies that work for you.

Use this space to write out your topic words the first time. Use your own paper for extra practice.

Rewrite here those you had most trouble with.

Fill in the gaps

Fill in the gaps with words from the **Topic spelling list**. Add ***s*** or ***ed*** to words where necessary.

1. Yesterday, I ____________ an absolute ____________—my best painting ever.
2. The teacher asked us to do a very quick ____________ of the scene.
3. We all did a ____________ of someone in the class and then guessed who each one was. We got most wrong. Some people drew funny ____________ in black and white.
4. It is difficult to get the right ____________ when painting a landscape.
5. I like paintings which are ____________, such as landscapes, portraits and ____________ pictures of fruit and flowers.
6. My sister prefers ____________ paintings full of weird shapes and images. She says the artists who do these are more ____________ than those who just paint as they see.
7. My parents and I have no ____________ ability at all, but my brother is fantastic at ____________ and painting.
8. Steffi and I entered the picture book competition together—I wrote the words and she did the ____________.
9. ____________ can be shaped out of many materials, for example clay, plaster, stone, timber, plastic or metal.
10. The ____________ at the ____________ displayed works of art from many schools in the area. Our school painted a giant ____________ on one wall.

Killer words

Study the words and tips and then write them without looking back.

audience	Break it into syllables to remember the ***i***: *AUD-I-ENCE*.	____________
surprise	It is ***sur****e* to ***sur****prise* you.	____________
invitation	Break it into syllables to remember the ***a***: *IN-VIT-A-TION*.	____________
appreciate	Chant out loud to remember this one!	____________
criticise	It contains *critic*. Write that first and you'll get the rest.	____________

Can you make up one sentence that includes all the **Killer words**? If you can't manage one, use two.

____

____

____

____

Looking at … *ure* words

Many common words end in ***ure***, e.g. *pict**ure***, *sculpt**ure***. Because the letters are not stressed, they can be tricky to spell.

1. Study these ***ure*** words. Look up the meanings of those you don't know.
2. When you think you know the spellings well, rewrite them in alphabetical order. Try not to keep looking back at the words—try to write them in one go.

picture	pressure	departure	furniture	caricature
agriculture	injure	leisure	treasure	torture
pasture	seizure	fracture	measure	azure
puncture	texture	signature	enclosure	culture

3. Which consonants often come before ***ure***? ______________________________
4. Choose five words to use in sentences—perhaps those you had to look up in the dictionary. Use your own paper.

Proofreading

Can you find the spelling mistakes in this student's writing?

Our class went into the sity last week to visit the Art Galery. I wasn't shore what to expeckt. I knew I woud see lots of pantings and sculpchures, and we did see lots of these. I liked the abstrackt pantings best becorse of the brilant colurs and desines, but most of the class perferred the reelistic ones—pitchers of landscapes and portrats of famose peeple. However, I was serprised to see furnitur, cloth, mettal and other strange matterials all twisted and moulded into funny forms. Our teacher explaned that this was all moddern art, and that artists used many matterials and tecknique these days to create their masterpeaces. We also saw some very colourfull grafiti in a spesial exibition. These pieces were absolutely huge, covering whole walls sometimes. Some of the graffiti included ilostrations and cartunes as well. They showed that graffiti art takes skil and artistick ability just like other kinds of art. I think we all apreciate art a lot more now after our excursion.

Vocabulary power

English uses many **words and expressions from foreign languages**. *Graffiti* is an example. *Graffiti* is an Italian word which derives from *graffio* meaning *scratch*. Sometimes when we take foreign words, we change the meaning a little. *Graffiti* now means drawings and words on walls and in other public places. Graffiti art is art in a graffiti style. Words from other languages can be difficult to spell.

1. Draw lines to match the foreign words and expressions on the left with their meanings on the right.

fete (French)	The first course in a meal.
prima donna (Italian)	A summary, usually of work experience.
rendezvous (French)	A meeting.
entree (French)	Something forbidden in a culture.
entrepreneur (French)	Speak or act without a script, improvise.
resume (French)	And so on.
ad lib (Latin)	A person who organises risky projects, especially in the entertainment business.
et cetera (Latin)	A person who gets emotional and causes difficulty.
taboo (Tongan)	An afternoon nap.
carafe (Italian)	A jug.
siesta (Italian)	A deep, circular cooking pan.
cafe (French)	A festival or form of entertainment, usually outdoors.
karaoke (Japanese)	A small restaurant.
wok (Chinese)	Singing along to recorded music.

2. Choose from the expressions above to complete the paragraph. Make the words into plurals if needed.

Dad awoke from his afternoon ________________ to find that he was running very late for the school ________________. His job was to help out in the art gallery ________________. He knew he was in big trouble because the woman in charge was a real ________________, and would be shouting and screaming because he was not already there. He rushed out of the house, forgetting the ________________ he had promised to bring for the cafe tables, and the ________________ to use in the kitchen. Mum had helped out last year, and she said this woman had terrified her. Mum said she was a local ________________, who had produced some very successful musical comedies. So she obviously had some good skills. Unfortunately for my Dad, being understanding about lateness was not one of them. He was not looking forward to his afternoon's work.

Read and learn

Read this information about Pablo Picasso, paying particular attention to the words in **bold**.

Pablo Picasso is probably the best known artist of the 20th century. He was an exceptionally **versatile** artist, **tackling** every **medium** imaginable including pencil, watercolour, oil and crayon, as well as sculpture in metal, plaster and stone. He also constructed artistic works out of **refuse** pulled out of rubbish bins.

Picasso was the son of an artist who earned his living teaching, drawing and working as a museum **curator**. He showed remarkable artistic talent and **potential** as a child. There is a story that when his father saw his son's work one day, he handed him his own **palette** and brushes and **vowed** never to paint again!

Picasso was born in Spain in 1881, but spent most of his time in Paris, which at that time was the centre of the art world. Picasso was one of the fathers of the **revolutionary** artistic movement known as Cubism.

His work changed in style over the years, but was always highly **original** in subject and artistic technique. Most people, when they think of the Picasso style, think of intense colours, **fragmented** figures and strange, **distorted,** flat shapes and surfaces. Picasso's influence over an entire generation of artists was overwhelming and is still being felt.

Now choose the answer that best matches the meaning of the words below as they are used in the text.

1 versatile	**a** able to use different styles	**b** quick to complete paintings
2 tackling	**a** holding a person down	**b** trying
3 medium	**a** material or technique	**b** average
4 refuse	**a** reject	**b** garbage
5 curator	**a** doctor or surgeon	**b** person in charge of gallery or museum
6 potential	**a** power	**b** ability to do something
7 palette	**a** tray of paints	**b** paintings
8 vowed	**a** promised	**b** refused
9 revolutionary	**a** completely new and different	**b** involving a war
10 original	**a** clever	**b** new
11 fragmented	**a** broken up	**b** small
12 distorted	**a** sad	**b** changed or twisted out of shape

Did you know?

The artist Michelangelo took four years to paint the ceiling of the Sistine Chapel in Rome. He planned and executed the gigantic painting alone, sometimes only by the light of a candle. He mostly had to paint leaning backwards or lying down. At the end of the four-year period, in 1512, he had created a monumental work of art, the like of which has not been seen again.

Puzzle

1 Which words from the unit are hiding the words below? Remember to look in the **Killer words** as well. One has been done for you.

a A kind of vehicle.	***car**toon* (car)	**b** Another word for *murder.*	________
c Another word for *characteristic.*	________	**d** A teacher or expert.	________
e The past tense of *eat.*	________	**f** A rodent.	________
g A word for *everyone.*	________	**h** Another word for *healthy.*	________
i The past tense of *bite.*	________	**j** Belonging to us.	________
k Another word for *go upwards.*	________	**l** A part of a bird.	________

2 Which words from the **Topic spelling list** are scrambled here?

a RUMAL	_ _ _ _ [ ]	**b** STICARTI	[ ] _ _ _ _ _ _ _
c QUETECHIN	_ _ _ _ [ ] _ _ _ _	**d** DAUIENCE	_ _ [ ] _ _ _ _ _
e FULLISK	[ ] _ _ _ _ _ _	**f** FULROCOLU	[ ] _ _ _ _ _ _ _ _
g BAACTSTR	[ ] _ _ _ _ _ _ _		
h REPIVESPECT	[ ] _ _ _ _ _ _ _ _ _ _	**i** PURSESIR	_ _ _ _ _ _ _ [ ]

The letters in the boxes will spell out something that is frequently the subject of paintings.

[ ] [ ] [ ] [ ] [ ] [ ] [ ] [ ] [ ]

Your turn to write

Interview a family member or friend about art. Here are some questions you could ask them, but you could also make up your own questions.

- What kind of paintings do you like? e.g. abstract, landscape, still life (flowers, etc.), portraits?
- Do you like sculpture? What kind (e.g. stone) and what subjects (e.g. the human body)?
- Do you like other art forms? e.g. sketches, drawings, etc.?
- Do you like visiting art galleries and art exhibitions? How often do you go? Where do you go?
- Are you artistic?
- Do you do any art or craft? What kind of thing do you do and what kinds of materials do you use?

Jot down their answers as they give them to you. Then write up your notes. Don't forget to revise and edit your work.

☞ Answers on pages 158–159

20 Wind, fire and rain

Quick fun

How many short words can you make from CATASTROPHE? I found 32.

Use this space to write out your topic words the first time. Use your own paper for extra practice.

Rewrite here those you had most trouble with.

Topic spelling list

weather	tsunami
calm	cyclone
bushfire	blowing
thunderstorm	freakish
lightning	tropical
hurricane	catastrophe
tornado	extreme
drought	conditions
blizzard	deluge
torrential	injury

Red hot hint

Be careful to avoid easy mistakes, e.g. don't drop the ***w*** or ***y*** when adding ***ing***: *blo**wing***, *destro**ying***.

Learn the words from the **Topic spelling list** using all the strategies you have learnt in this book.

Fill in the gaps

Fill in the gaps with words from the **Topic spelling list**. You might need to change the word endings.

1. The weather ____________ are too dangerous to go any further.
2. A meteorologist is someone who studies and then forecasts the ____________.
3. Many polar explorers have perished in the ____________ weather conditions in the Arctic and Antarctic. Some have been caught in the terrible ____________, which sometimes start up with little warning.
4. It is vital to stay ____________ if you are caught in a ____________ weather situation.
5. The ____________ which struck countries around the Indian Ocean in December 2004 took over 280 000 lives. Many thousands more lost their homes or suffered serious ____________.
6. Farmers in many countries spend many years struggling with ____________.
7. ____________, ____________ and ____________ are all kinds of violent wind storms.
8. Monsoons are periods of heavy rain which occur in hot, ____________ countries. They can bring ____________ to villagers living in coastal areas.
9. Some ____________ are started by ____________ strikes during severe ____________.

Killer words

Study the words and the tips and then write them without looking back.

whether	Remember: it is a ***wh*** word like ***wh***ere and ***wh***at.	____________
accident	Underline the double **c** and remember it.	____________
scared	Remember: *I **care** if you are s**care**d.*	____________
flood	Learn with *blood*.	____________
damage	Use a spelling pronunciation: *dam-AGE*.	____________

Can you make up one sentence that includes all the **Killer words**? If you can't manage one, use two.

____

____

____

____

Looking at … silent consonants

English uses many **silent consonants**. Look at these examples (the silent consonants are **bold**):

ca**l**m **w**rong bom**b** lis**t**en **k**nock rei**g**n **h**our autum**n** **p**salm ai**s**le

1. Underline the silent consonant in each word below. Then rewrite them, grouping the ones containing the same silent consonant together. (Use your own paper.)

foreign	climb	subtle	doubt	gnash	gnome
honour	gnarled	gnaw	folk	knowledge	salmon
honest	solemn	moisten	damn	design	resign
heir	condemn	psychology	knuckle	column	knot
wrestle	wreak	receipt	psychic	fasten	wreck

2. Which words from the list mean the same as these words and expressions? Use your dictionary if needed.

a Give up. ____________ b A small creature like an elf. ____________

c Fight. ____________ d Destroy. ____________

e Strange, unknown. ____________ f People. ____________

g A bone on the hand. ____________ h Not obvious. ____________

i Rough and twisted. ____________ j Bite or chew constantly. ____________

3. Which words complete these common expressions?

a to g _ _ _ _ your teeth with rage b the son and h _ _ _

c to w _ _ _ _ havoc d a garden g _ _ _ _

e a s _ _ _ _ _ hint f w _ _ _ _ _ _ _ with a problem

g to have a k _ _ _ in your stomach h to c _ _ _ _ _ _ _ to death

i to give your s _ _ _ _ _ promise j I swear on my h _ _ _ _ _.

Proofreading

Can you correct this student's unit spelling test? If a word is incorrect, write the correct spelling next to it. Did you get 100% correct?

thundderstorm	____________	blizard	____________	cyclone	____________
carm	____________	acident	____________	bloing	____________
bushfire	____________	doubt	____________	freakish	____________
lightening	____________	honour	____________	catastrophe	____________
hurricane	____________	tornado	____________	extream	____________
scared	____________	damidge	____________	reck	____________
flood	____________	torrenshal	____________	colum	____________
drout	____________	tsunami	____________	receit	____________

Vocabulary power

1 There are many adjectives that we use to talk about **the weather and nature**. However, we don't always use the same adjectives with the same nouns. For example, we say *strong wind* but *heavy rain*. We don't say *heavy wind* or *strong rain*. We say *a fierce storm* or *wind* or *fire*, but we don't say *fierce rain*.

Which of the adjectives in the box can go with the nouns below? Some adjectives will go with more than one.

Hint: Say them out loud before you write them. Some will probably sound right and others will probably sound wrong.

flooding	heavy	driving	freak	gale-force	blazing	lashing
ferocious	dazzling	pouring	steady	stiff	blustery	torrential
strong	howling	raging	fierce	severe	brilliant	violent

fire ______________________________

rain ______________________________

wind ______________________________

storm ______________________________

sunshine ______________________________

2 Now look at these adjectives which can all go before the noun *weather*. Put them into three groups: very good weather, ordinary weather, very bad weather.

gloomy	dismal	fine	reasonable	atrocious	miserable	foul
glorious	superb	nasty	lovely	dreadful	great	terrible
lousy	appalling	fair	grim	vile	stupendous	brilliant

Very good weather

Ordinary weather

Very bad weather

Very good weather	Ordinary weather	Very bad weather

Read and learn

The best way to learn new words and new ways of expressing ideas is by reading. Take time when you read to look at new and interesting words and expressions.

The extract below is from a story about a flood. It includes many descriptive words and expressions to describe the wind, the rain and the young boy battling to get home.

> Barney stopped under the Hanging Tree and looked out toward the river, now only a dim dark line of trees and maybe the cliff-line of the other side. The air was heavy with scudding, swirling water and battering wind and he could not toss aside the feeling that he was peering down through a stormy sea at a drowned valley. He tried to remember how the valley had been—a week ago, a few days ago, a few *hours* ago.
>
> A howling gust of wind bent the willow and tore Barney from its trunk. Barney staggered against the wind for a few paces, his fingers touching the ground, then he realised that if he stopped struggling the gust would blow him home. He turned, felt the wind pressing hard against his back, and began to totter down the hill. He grinned and watched his feet shuffle a long way ahead of his body. His raincoat flattened against his body and he became a walking, running sail.
>
> Barney hunched against the sleet and plodded along the road. He did not look back. Everything was grey now, grey, turbulent and frightened. To his right, a line of trees marked a raised bank of the river and he could almost hear it hissing past their roots. A ramshackle timber house beside a rusty tower had already been abandoned and the flat paddocks were turning into a lake.
>
> The wind punched him in the side and he stepped sideways to recover his balance. He knew what was going to happen tonight and the knowledge dried his mouth.
>
>

1. Write down at least three words and expressions used to describe the rain or water. ______

______

2. Write down at least three words and expressions used to describe the action of the wind.

______

______

3. Write down at least three words and expressions used to describe the movements of the boy as he struggles against the wind and rain.

______

______

4. Which words in paragraph 3 best describe the overall air and atmosphere? ______

______

Do you know these idioms?

These idioms all use **weather** images. Can you work them out?

weather/ride out the storm	come hail, rain or shine	it never rains but it pours
be right as rain	the calm before the storm	the eye of the storm
a storm in a teacup	take the place by storm	catch wind of something

Puzzle

Use words from the word lists in this unit to complete the crossword.

Across

3 Another word for *flood*.
5 The state of things, the situation.
8 A violent cyclonic tropical storm.
12 I don't know __________ I will or won't.
14 Often used to describe an old and twisted tree.
16 If you don't have 19 across, you might experience this.
17 You might feel this in a thunderstorm.
18 Rain, wind, hail, sunshine … all of it.
19 You need this to forecast the weather.
20 Heavy, constant, gushing.

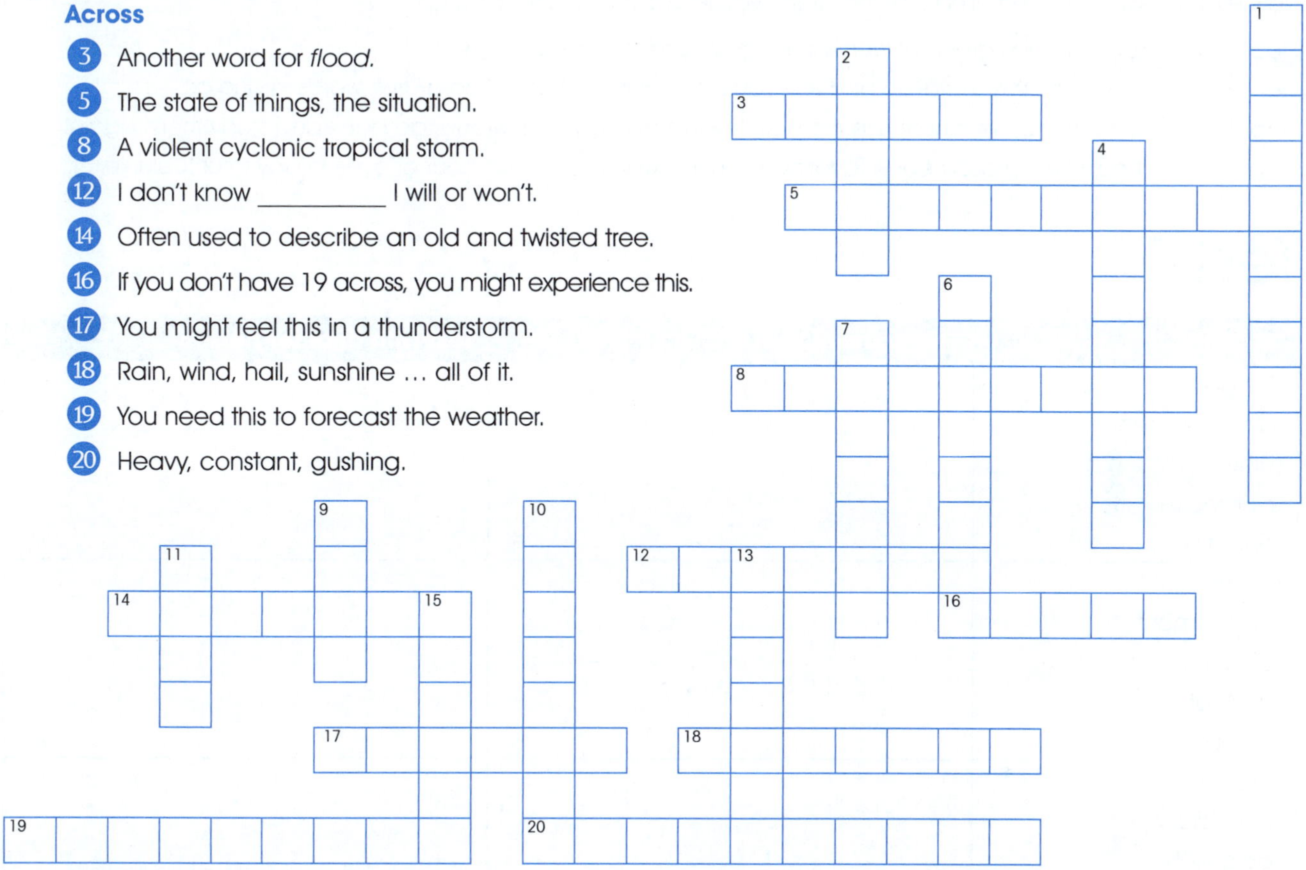

Down

1 Partly rhymes with *apostrophe*.
4 Can be described as *forked* or *sheet*.
7 The opposite of *flood*.
10 Bad weather makes this more likely.
13 Extraordinary, beyond the limits.
2 Take away one letter and get something we can't live without.
6 A violent snowstorm.
9 Another word for *people*.
11 A measure of wind speed.
15 Harm or injury.

Your turn to write

Choose one of the following tasks. Remember to do a rough draft first, and to revise and edit your writing.

1 Write a poem about the weather or a natural disaster. It might be about a storm, a flood, a hurricane, a drought or a bushfire. Try to use some words from the unit, including the **Vocabulary power** and **Read and learn** sections.

OR

2 Write a short recount about an experience in an extreme weather situation—perhaps walking or riding home from school, or being at home with your family during a frightening situation. Again, try to use words from the unit.

☞Answers on pages 159–160

Review 4

Now let's see what you remember of the words you learnt in Units 16–20.

Step 1 Look at each group of words in the test to revise the spellings.

Step 2 Cover the five words up and test yourself (column 2). Try to do all five words in one go.

Step 3 Write your score out of 5 in the box. If you got any words wrong, go back and study them again.

Step 4 If possible, ask someone to test you on the words later—an hour or even a day later (column 3).

Test 1

Study	Test yourself	Test with another person
bargain advertisement aisle millionaire quantity	/5	/5
quality department unique budget suitable	/5	/5
receipt necessary essentials extravagant money	/5	/5
buy bought paid persuade happen	/5	/5
human urban woman bargain captain	/5	/5
examine medicine climate pollution chemical	/5	/5
	Total score = out of 30	Total score = out of 30

Test 2

Study	Test yourself	Test with another person
garbage destroy awareness environment community	/5	/5
recycle behaviour responsibility choose chosen	/5	/5
choice amongst neighbour known drawn	/5	/5
forgotten caught heard meant said	/5	/5
caught culture social society traditional	/5	/5
modern language familiar foreign attitude	/5	/5
	Total score = out of 30	Total score = out of 30

Test 3

Study	Test yourself	Test with another person
acceptance prejudice difference fascinating behaviour	/5	/5
recognise exist exercise exhausted execute	/5	/5
expect extreme exhibit excellent exception	/5	/5
excuse artistic realistic sculpture illustration	/5	/5
skilful colourful create masterpiece technique	/5	/5
perspective portrait audience surprise invitation	/5	/5
	Total score = out of 30	Total score = out of 30

Test 4

Study	Test yourself	Test with another person
appreciate pressure texture treasure calm	/5	/5
bushfire thunderstorm lightning hurricane tornado	/5	/5
drought blizzard torrential tsunami cyclone	/5	/5
blowing freakish catastrophe extreme doubt	/5	/5
deluge accident scared flood damage	/5	/5
knowledge psychology honest wreck resign	/5	/5
	Total score = out of 30	Total score = out of 30

Which word?

1. She was asked to ______________ the award on behalf of the class. (*accept, except*)
2. Everyone ________________ Maria attended the ceremony. (*accept, except*)
3. We chanted the spellings ______________ until we knew them. (*allowed, aloud*)
4. We weren't _________________ to play near the new building works. (*allowed, aloud*)
5. There was a huge _________________ in the wall. (*hole, whole*)
6. The ______________ class went on the excursion. (*hole, whole*)

Congratulations! You've made it to the last test. I hope you feel more confident about your spelling now. But learning to spell is only useful if you write, so try to write as much as you can, won't you?

☞Answers on page 159

Word list

abbeys
abilities
abstract
absurd
accelerate
accept
acceptance
accident
accountant
achieve
action
activities
activity
actor
actually
addition
adult
advance
adventures
advertisement
afterwards
again
against
agent
agree
agriculture
aisle
all
allowed
almost
aloud
although
always
amongst
amount
ancestors
ancient
angel
anniversary
annual
annually
answer
appear
applause
appliances
appreciate
aquatic
architect
area
argue
argument
armies
artistic
assistant
assisted
ate
atlas
atmosphere
attacked
attention
attitude
attraction
attractive
audience
average
award
awareness
azure
backwards
bacon
balance
bald
bargain
battle
battled
baulk
beautiful
beauty
because
beforehand
beginning
behaviour
belief
believe
between
billabong
biography
birth
birthdays
blew
blizzard
blonde
blood
blow
blowing
blown
bodies
body
born
bought
bread
break
breath
breathe
brief
broke
broken
budget
build
builder
bulletin
buoys
burglar
burn
bushfire
business
busy
button
buy
cabin
calm
camped
can't
captain
cardboard
carefully
caricature
cartoon
castle
catalogue
catastrophe
catch
caught
ceiling
celebrate
celebration
cellar
cells
census
central
century
ceremony
certain
certainly
chalk
changed
character
charming
cheer
chemical
chemicals
chemist
chief
childhood
children
choice
choose
chosen
church
circle
circular
circulation
cities
citizen

citrus
city
civilisation
cliff
climate
climb
cloth
clothes
collect
colony
coloured
colourful
column
comedian
commemorate
commotion
community
competition
completely
compost
comprehension
conclusion
condemn
conditions
confusion
conquer
conquered
conserve
continent
conversation
convoys
coral
could
countries
courageous
crawl
create
creek
crimson
criticise
crooked
crossed
crowd
cruel
cultural
culture
curl
curly-haired
current
curt
curtain
curve
customs
cyclone
damage
damn
dangerous
dead
deaf
death
decade
decimal
decision
decoys
decrease
definitely
deluge
demon
demonstration
department
departure
depth
description
desert
design
designer
destroy
diagram
die
died
difference
different
digit
dilute
dimension
direction
disagree
disappear
discount
discovered
display
disturb
divide
division
doctor
does
doesn't
dolphin
doubt
dragon
draw
drawing
drawn
dread
drew
drive
driven
drought
drove
dungeon
during
dwarf
dye
eastern
eat
eaten
Egypt
eighteenth
eighth
either
eldest
eleventh
emperor
empire
enclosure
energy
engine
enough
entertainment
environment
equal
equipment
erosion
especially
essentials
estimate
even
exactly
exam
examine
example
exceed
excel
excellent
except
exception
excess
exchange
excite
excitement
exciting
excursion
excuse
execute
exercise
exhale
exhausted
exhibit
exhibition
exile
exist
exit
exotic
expect
expel
expensive
experiences
experiment
expert
explored
explosion
extension
extinct
extract
extravagant
extreme

extremely
factories
falter
familiar
families
famine
famous
fancy
fascinate
fascinating
fasten
fauna
favourite
feast
feather
feminine
festival
fiction
field
fierce
fifteenth
fifth
fir
firm
first
firstly
flashed
flew
flirt
flood
flora
flown
fly
folk
followed
foreign
forest
forgot
forgotten
fortnight
forwards
fountain
fourteenth
fourth

fraction
fracture
frankly
freakish
freckles
friends
frizzy
furniture
further
future
gala
gallery
garbage
gem
generally
generous
genes
genetic
genius
gently
geography
germ
gesture
giant
girder
gnarled
gnash
gnaw
gnome
goblin
goes
gorgeous
govern
governed
government
gradually
graffiti
graph
grew up
grief
guessed
guest
gurgle
guys

gymnastics
gypsy
handsome
happen
happily
harbour
hasn't
haste
hated
he'd
head
health
healthy
hear
heard
heart
heaven
heavy
height
heir
hemisphere
hero
heroes
heroine
hid
hidden
hide
history
hobbies
hole
holiday
honest
honour
horizon
hour
huge
human
hundredth
hurricane
hurried
hurrying
I'll
I'm
illustration

image
immediately
information
initially
injure
injury
instead
instructions
instructor
interest
invade
invaded
invitation
island
it's
javelin
jealousy
jockeys
journalist
journeys
kingdom
knew
knight
knot
know
knowledge
known
knuckle
ladies
lagoon
landscape
language
large
lasted
latitude
laughter
leather
leave
left
leisure
lemon
lessen
lesson
librarian

lightning
liked
liquid
listen
lived
location
longitude
lovely
lunge
magic
magnificent
manager
margin
marine
married
masculine
masterpiece
material
meadow
mean
meant
meanwhile
measure
mechanic
medicine
metal
method
millennium
millionaire
minus
minute
mirth
mobile
modern
moisten
moment
money
monkeys
monthly
motionless
mountain
movement
multiplication
multiplied
mural
murder
murmur
muscle
muscular
musician
napkin
nation
national park
natural
nature
nearly
necessary
negative
neighbour
neither
nervous
niece
nineteenth
ninetieth
ninth
normally
northern
notice
nowadays
occasion
occur
ocean
oceanic
often
ogre
olive-skinned
once
opinion
ordinary
origin
originally
orphan
our
ozone layer
paddock
paid
parade
parents
particularly
parties
passed
past
pasture
pattern
peace
peaceful
peasant
people
percentage
perhaps
period
personally
perspective
persuade
persuasion
photographer
physical
picture
piece
pier
pierce
pigsties
pioneer
plastic
pleasant
pleasure
plump
plus
polar
pollution
portrait
position
positive
possible
possibly
prejudice
present
pressure
pretty
priest
prince
princess
probable
probably
procedure
procession
professor
protection
psychic
psychology
puncture
purchase
purchases
purple
purse
quadrant
qualities
quality
quantity
quarry
quarter
quays
quiet
quirky
quite
range
rapidly
rather
reached
ready
realistic
really
reason
rebellion
receipt
recent
recently
recite
recognise
recycle
recycled
reduce
region
reign
reigned
relief

relieve
religion
remember
remembered
remembering
rescue
resign
resources
respect
responsibility
revision
reward
rhythm
ridden
ride
river
rode
rotten
rubbish
rural
said
salmon
salt
saved
say
scald
scared
scarred
scenery
schedule
science
scientist
scissors
sculpture
season
second
secretary
seizure
senses
sentence
service
settled
settlement
settler

seventeenth
seventh
shake
shaken
shallow
shan't
she's
shield
shirt
shook
should
show
showed
shown
shriek
siege
signature
similar
sincerely
sir
sixteenth
sixth
skeleton
sketch
skilful
skill
skirmish
skirt
slender
slogan
small
smoothly
social
society
soldier
solemn
southern
spacious
special
spectacular
spectators
spies
spread
squabble

squad
squadron
squalid
squash
swat
squat
squatter
squirm
squirt
station
stationary
steady
stealthy
stir
stomach
straight
strait
strays
stream
strength
sturdy
subtle
subtraction
suddenly
suitable
supplies
surely
surf
surface
surgeon
surname
surprise
suspension
swab
swaddle
swam
swamp
swap
swarm
swarthy
swiftly
swim
swirl
swollen

swum
tail
tale
talk
tartan
technique
television
temperature
tension
tenth
terribly
territories
texture
their
there
they're
thief
third
thirsty
thirteenth
thirtieth
thirty
though
thought
thousand
thousandth
thread
threat
threw
through
thunderstorm
tidal
tier
timber
to
token
tomorrow
too
tornado
torrent
torrential
torture
total
totally

towards
tower
toxic
tradition
traditional
tread
treasure
tributary
tropical
tsunami
turkey
turn
twaddle
twelfth
twenties
twentieth
twice
twirl
two
unique
urban
urchin
value
velocity
version
viewpoint
village
villain
virgin
virtue
vision
wadding
waft
wall
wallabies
wallop
wallow
wan
wander
wandered
want
war
ward
warden
wardrobe
warm
warn
warp
warrant
warrior
wart
was
wash
wasn't
waste
watch
watt
wattle
weak
wealth
weapon
wear
wearing
weather
week
weight
were
western
wharf
what
whatever
wheat
wheel
when
whenever
where
whereas
wherever
whether
which
whichever
while
whimper
whip
whirl
whisker
whisper
whistle
white
who
who's
whole
whom
whose
why
wicked
width
wilderness
witch
wizard
woman
won
won't
wore
worked
worn
would
would've
wreak
wreck
wrestle
wriggle
years
yesterday
you'd
you'll
you're
youngest
your
zone

Answers

1 Life stories (pages 2–7)

Quick fun (page 2)

RAN, PEAR, PARE, RENT, SENT, PANTS, STAR, STEP, TRAP, TREND, GRAND, PARENTS, AND, PAD, PAT, SAP, TAP, RAP, NAP, STAND, STRAND, STRAP, PAR, SPAR, NEAR, DEAR, GEAR, TEAR, SEAR, STARE, DARE, RARE

Fill in the gaps (page 3)

1 famous, born, lived **2** children **3** years **4** originally, ancestors **5** grew up **6** parents, adventures/experiences **7** biography **8** married **9** eldest, youngest **10** death, birth **11** childhood, adult, adventures/experiences

Word scramble (page 3)

1 MARRIED **2** FAMOUS **3** EXPERIENCES **4** CHILDREN **5** ORIGINALLY **6** PARENTS **7** ADVENTURES **8** ANCESTORS

Killer words (page 4)

People, remember, remembering, friends, remembered

Looking at … short e sound spelt *ea* (pages 4–5)

1 These words can be grouped together:
- head, tread, dead, spread, bread, dread, thread
- steady, ready
- health, wealth, stealthy
- death, breath
- feather, weather, leather
- pleasant, peasant
- treasure, measure, pleasure
- heaven, heavy.

You might also group: weather, weapon; thread, threat; death, deaf.

2

a	D	**E**	**A**	D				
b	D	R	**E**	**A**	D			
c	H	**E**	**A**	L	T	H		
d	J	**E**	**A**	L	O	U	S	Y
e	P	L	**E**	**A**	S	A	N	T
f	T	R	**E**	**A**	S	U	R	E
g	S	T	**E**	**A**	L	T	H	
h	B	R	**E**	**A**	T	H		
i	R	**E**	**A**	D	Y			
j	D	**E**	**A**	F				

(**c** W**EA**LTH also possible)

Proofreading (page 5)

My great-grandparents came to Australia from Greece in 1950. My great-grandfather says he remembers the trip here by boat, and how sad he was to be leaving the small town where he was born and grew up, and where his ancestors had lived and died. He was the youngest of twelve children, and so he was leaving behind many brothers and sisters as well as friends. My great-grandmother was sad to leave her parents, but she was very happy to come to a new country. They were not wealthy people and so when they arrived, life was very difficult. They often tell us about their experiences and adventures when they first arrived and all the mistakes they made with English. We love to hear them talk about my grandfather's childhood.

Vocabulary power (page 6)

1 brothers and sisters – siblings; children – offspring; teenager – adolescent; happy – content; ancestors – forebears; bring up – raise; yearly – annual; marriage – union; died – passed away; motherly – maternal; achievement – feat; origin – birthplace; time – period; ambition – goal; fatherly – paternal; remembrance – memory

Read and learn (pages 6–7)

1 **a** i **b** ii **c** i **d** i **e** ii **f** i

Puzzle (page 7)

B	E	E	U	Q	V	E	A	F	A	M	O	U	S	D	E	A	T	H	S	A	R	G	F	P	A	R	E	N	T	S	R
E	X	E	N	F	B	A	N	S	W	E	A	L	T	H	R	C	Y	A	T	U	Y	R	O	L	I	V	E	D	O	M	E
T	P	E	O	P	L	E	Q	O	P	N	S	E	Y	O	U	D	E	A	F	W	O	E	O	M	E	B	I	R	T	H	L
A	E	B	W	C	A	E	C	H	I	L	D	R	E	N	M	A	B	Q	S	E	U	W	M	A	E	B	W	C	A	Z	R
F	R	I	E	N	D	N	A	E	E	L	D	E	S	T	P	I	R	B	T	A	N	E	P	E	A	S	A	N	T	M	L
O	I	M	K	R	O	X	T	A	V	P	L	M	Y	E	A	R	S	E	M	P	G	F	E	R	S	S	N	N	I	R	E
H	E	A	L	T	H	T	H	V	O	Q	T	H	R	E	A	T	C	R	D	O	E	B	B	I	O	G	R	A	P	H	Y
E	N	O	V	A	B	S	Q	E	P	R	M	X	L	F	G	H	R	M	I	N	S	J	I	A	D	U	L	T	L	A	M
N	C	P	C	Y	O	E	O	N	A	A	D	V	E	N	T	U	R	E	E	U	T	G	M	R	E	M	E	M	B	E	R
M	E	O	N	O	R	V	X	R	Q	M	C	H	I	L	D	H	O	O	D	G	O	R	I	G	I	N	A	L	L	Y	D
R	S	A	N	U	N	H	M	A	R	R	I	E	D	G	O	L	I	O	B	A	N	C	E	S	T	O	R	S	N	N	Q

2 The working world (pages 8–13)

Quick fun (page 8)

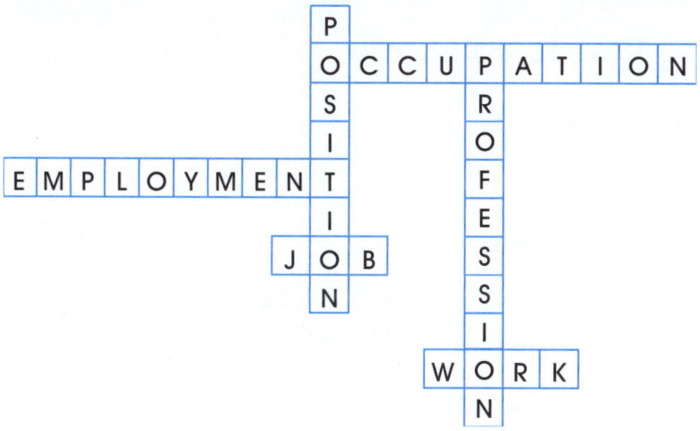

Fill in the gaps (page 9)

1 librarian **2** assistant **3** doctor, chemist **4** instructor **5** journalist **6** accountant **7** photographer **8** builder, architect, actor **9** secretaries **10** mechanic **11** comedian **12** professors

Looking at ... *wh* words (page 10)

1 **a** who's **b** who **c** where **d** why **e** whose **f** whisper **g** which **h** what **i** when **j** whom **k** wherever **l** whether **m** whereas **n** wheel

Looking at ... apostrophe of possession (page 10)

1 **a** I was allowed to stay in the mechanics' workroom all day. It was great to watch them at work.
b The scientist's prize was $50 000. He will use it for research.
c The accountants' lunch took place yesterday. More than 100 people attended.
d The journalists' stories were not published. Even worse, they lost their jobs.

2 **a** The two professors agreed with each other.
b My doctor's surgery is not far away.
c The young musician's van was broken into. He lost everything.
d The builders were late starting work.

Proofreading (page 11)

When I grow up, I would like to have an interesting and busy job. My big brother used to say the same thing when he was little and now he works as a landscape designer. He travels all over the country, wherever people want him. I don't think I would want to work outside all the time like him, but it would be good to find something which always interested me. At the moment I am thinking I might be a journalist because I like writing, although Mum says I will have to improve my spelling if I want to spend my life writing. My father thinks that I should be a scientist because that is what he always wanted to be.

Vocabulary power (page 11)

1 **a** editor **b** historian **c** mathematician **d** optician **e** electrician **f** florist **g** machinist **h** receptionist **i** technician **j** specialist

2 bricklayer, supervisor, kitchenhand, sergeant, lawyer, dentist, jackaroo, pilot, soldier, physiotherapist, solicitor, manufacturer, bookkeeper, hairdresser, carpenter, computer programmer

Dictionary search (page 12)

meteorologist = weather; ornithologist = birds; archaeologist = past ways of life; paleontologist = past animal and plant life; vulcanologist = volcanoes; oceanologist = oceans; futurologist = the future; anthropologist = development of humans; cryptologist = codes and ciphers; genealogist = family histories; herpetologist = reptiles and amphibians; seismologist = earthquakes

Read and learn (page 12)

turnkey: guarded prisoners
alchemist: turned ordinary metals into gold
bill poster: put up signs and advertisements
fleshmonger: sold meat
fowler: farmed hens, ducks and other poultry
ashman: took away the rubbish
crier: announced the important events in a town
charwoman: cleaned houses for others
cutler: sold and sharpened knives
ankle beater: helped drive cattle to market

Puzzle (page 13)

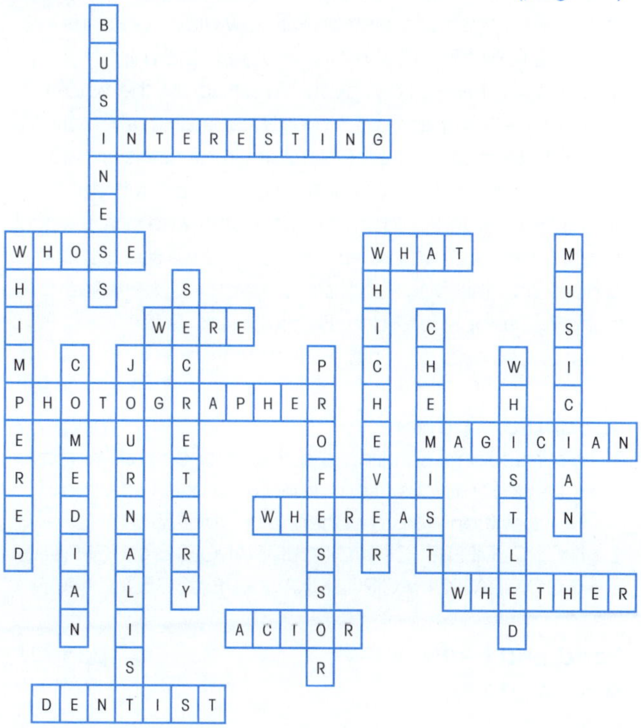

3 Around the globe (pages 14–19)

Quick fun (page 14)
1 EQUATOR
2 TROPIC OF CANCER
3 TROPIC OF CAPRICORN
4 ANTARCTIC CIRCLE
5 ARCTIC CIRCLE
6 INTERNATIONAL DATE LINE

Fill in the gaps (page 15)
1 countries **2** cities **3** continent, island **4** longitude, latitude, ocean **5** tropics, temperatures **6** desert, mountains **7** atlas **8** atmosphere **9** hemispheres **10** Circle, polar **11** zones **12** horizon

Looking at plurals of words ending in *y* (page 16)
1 birthdays, decoys, families, spies, bodies, monkeys, jockeys, supplies, quays, armies, qualities, ladies, parties, activities, guys, journeys, factories, territories
2 **a** buoys **b** convoys **c** pigsties **d** strays **e** abbeys **f** hobbies **g** wallabies **h** subways **i** abilities
3 **a** supplies, convoys **b** ladies, hobbies, strays **c** spies, activities **d** jockeys, abilities

Proofreading (page 17)
Brazil is the largest and most populous country in South America. You might be surprised to hear that in total area it is bigger than Australia and only slightly smaller than the United States. It covers a vast area from above the Equator in the north to below the Tropic of Cancer in the south. Brazil has varied terrain with low plains and hills in some regions, and mountains in others. The mighty Amazon River flows from east to west across the whole country. The temperature is mostly tropical, particularly in the rainforests of the north. Brazil's capital city is Brasilia, but its largest and most well-known cities are Rio de Janeiro and Sao Paolo. It doesn't matter where you travel in Brazil, because wherever you go, you will see sights that amaze and thrill you. What's more, you will meet the friendliest people on Earth. Be prepared for the experiences and adventures of a lifetime.

Vocabulary power (page 17)
1 **a** semicolon **b** semifinal **c** semidetached **d** semiquaver **e** semi-conscious **f** semi-trailer (you often see *semi* words written with a hyphen, e.g. *semi-final*)
2 **a** CIRCUMFERENCE **b** CIRCUMSTANCES **c** COOPERATE **d** CONTRADICT **e** CIRCUMNAVIGATE **f** COEDUCATION

Read and learn (page 18)
a i **b** i **c** ii **d** ii **e** ii **f** i

Puzzle (page 19)
alas, done, tin, dessert, main, Iceland, gratitude, count, motion, molar, legion, scarcity, atmospheric, chorizo

4 Time to celebrate (pages 20–25)

Quick fun (page 20)
FIREWORKS

Word scramble (page 20)
1 CELEBRATE **2** APPLAUSE **3** COMMEMORATE **4** HOLIDAY **5** PROCESSION **6** CEREMONY **7** ANNUAL **8** SPECTATOR

Fill in the gaps (page 21)
1 celebrated, anniversary **2** crowd, parade/procession **3** entertainment **4** annually **5** applause **6** commemorated **7** tradition **8** display **9** cheers, parade/procession **10** holiday **11** celebration, feast **12** festivals

Looking at … *tion* words (page 22)
1 **a** DIRECTION **b** NATION **c** FICTION **d** COMMOTION **e** STATION **f** LOCATION **g** ATTRACTION **h** INFORMATION
3 Here is one interpretation: the poem is about a boy who sees someone with a punk hairdo and decides to get his hair cut in the same way. His parents at first are horrified but then ask him to change it just a little. He does and everyone is happy.
Punctuation is spelt *punktuation* because the poem is about a 'punk' hairdo.

Proofreading (page 23)
SPECIAL event—come celebrate with us
Attractions for young and old: fireworks, bands and a Grand Parade
All day entertainment: **GLADSTONE GALA DAY**
To commemorate the day the railway came to Gladstone
All spectators get free entry to train exibition
Children under five get a free balloon and train ride
When? Saturday 12th July (second weekend of the school holidays)
Where? Main Street, Gladstone
Just follow the crowds!

Vocabulary power (page 23)
1 **a** remember **b** memory **c** memento **d** memorable
2 **a** spectacles **b** spectacular **c** inspect **d** respect
3 annual, annually, anniversary. The word root ***ann*** means *year.*

Dictionary search (page 23)
Examples of ***mem*** words: memorial, memoir, memorabilia, memorandum, memorise. Examples of ***spect*** words: spectrum, spectacle, spectator, spectral, spectrograph, spectroscope.

Read and learn (page 24)

1 a i b i c ii d ii e i f ii g i

2 A volcano; because it conveys the sudden and noisy way the town changes at festival time (like a volcano).

Puzzle (page 25)

1 PARAD**E** 2 **C**OMMEMORATE 3 **T**RADITION
4 HO**L**IDAY 5 CELE**B**RATE 6 C**R**OWD
7 **A**NNUALLY 8 CH**E**ER 9 SURPR**I**SE
10 C**O**MPETITIO**N**

ECTLBRAEION ⟶ CELEBRATION

5 In my opinion (pages 26–31)

Fill in the gaps (page 27)

1 opinion 2 perhaps, really 3 argue, disagree 4 Surely, believe 5 totally, argument 6 agree, negative 7 possible, probably 8 possibly, reasons 9 positive, Personally

Killer words (page 27)

thought, could, would, should, against, again

Looking at words ending in *-ly* (page 28)

1 a initially b definitely c normally d actually e particularly f sincerely g frankly h terribly i generally j completely

Looking at … proverbs (pages 28–29)

1 a heads b wise c blood d words e perfect f hand g link h book i cat j pudding k Beggars l cake

2 a g b d c k d a

Proofreading (page 29)

Dear Editor

I am writing to give my opinion about the plan to build more houses in the bushland behind Murray Road. I can give you three reasons why you should not do this. Firstly, I don't want to see all those kangaroos, wallabies, frogs and birds being killed just for houses. Surely they can build them somewhere else. Personally, I think the animals have the right to the land—they were there first. Secondly, I really think that it will make the traffic worse on that road. I can't believe you have not thought about this—so why would you do it? Thirdly, I totally agree with Koby Bruin who wrote to your paper last week. He gave a very good argument for not building: the residents in the new houses will be in danger from bushfires.

Vocabulary power (pages 29–30)

You might find these words for:

agree: concur, assent, see eye to eye, shake hands

argument: quarrel, dispute, difference, controversy, altercation, conflict

disagree: differ, dissent, dispute, bicker, wrangle, argue

Read and learn (page 30)

a separate b enthusiastic c take over d not as good as people say e makes easier f too much g doubtful h possibility

Puzzle (page 30)

R	P	O	S	S	I	B	L	Y	X	X	I	P	N	U	K
F	P	N	P	E	R	H	A	P	S	H	O	R	O	H	Y
B	O	E	V	H	S	U	R	E	L	Y	P	O	T	R	I
C	S	G	I	Y	J	G	K	D	A	A	I	B	Q	B	S
E	I	A	E	R	Y	Z	Z	R	R	D	N	A	F	R	H
L	T	T	W	P	E	H	E	G	C	I	I	B	K	E	O
Y	I	I	P	W	M	U	U	K	Q	S	O	L	T	A	U
C	V	V	O	R	T	P	S	W	T	A	N	Y	A	L	L
E	E	E	I	O	E	O	H	O	U	G	S	I	R	L	D
R	T	U	N	N	Y	S	W	U	N	R	M	R	G	Y	A
T	H	T	T	P	J	S	P	L	S	E	I	E	U	Y	Q
A	O	M	K	Y	K	I	I	D	G	E	R	A	M	W	P
I	U	J	F	I	W	B	K	X	N	J	X	S	E	J	X
N	G	M	E	J	E	L	A	R	G	U	E	O	N	I	S
L	H	E	E	X	J	E	K	G	R	S	O	N	T	P	F
Y	T	O	T	A	L	L	Y	B	A	G	A	I	N	S	T

Review 1 (pages 32–35)

Which word? (page 35)

1 whether 2 who's 3 where 4 which

6 Life through the ages (pages 36–41)

Quick fun (page 36)

1 VIKINGS 2 AZTECS 3 ROMANS 4 EGYPTIANS 5 GREEKS

Fill in the gaps

1 colonies 2 century 3 settlers 4 warriors, invaded 5 battles, War 6 reigned 7 rebellion 8 ancient 9 period 10 conquered, Peaceful 11 emperors

Killer words (page 37)

1 du**ring** 2 th**rough** 3 discove**red** 4 k**now**n 5 g**over**nment or disc**over**ed

Looking at … *or* sound spelt *a* and *ar* (page 38)

1 The ***or*** sound is usually spelt ***ar*** when following a ***w***, ***sw*** or ***kwa*** (***qu***) sound.
The ***or*** sound is usually spelt ***a*** in front of a double ***l*** or an ***l*** + consonant.

2 **a** wharf **b** war **c** talk **d** warden **e** wardrobe **f** scald **g** warn **h** award **i** falter **j** almost **k** all **l** warm **m** swarthy **n** dwarf **o** always **p** warp **q** ward **r** baulk

Looking at ... regular past tenses (pages 38–39)

1

invaded (id)	settled (d)	conquered (d)
battled (d)	reached (t)	crossed (t)
saved (d)	reigned (d)	hurried (d)
flashed (t)	attacked (t)	married (d)
lasted (id)	explored (d)	governed (d)
changed (d)	assisted (id)	liked (t)
hated (id)	camped (t)	

3 **a** danced, dancing **b** ruled, ruling **c** served, serving **d** waved, waving **e** dined, dining **f** chased, chasing **g** argued, arguing **h** loved, loving

Puzzle (page 39)

1 HISTORIAN **2** RATTLE **3** BELL **4** UMPIRE **5** RESIGN **6** WARP **7** CENT **8** SNEER **9** QUERY **10** CENTURION

Proofreading (page 40)

From the seventh to the fifth century BC, Rome was ruled by kings. Then the Romans set up a republic and elected their leaders. This worked well for many years until a powerful general called Julius Caesar took control in 45 BC. He was murdered five years later, and his nephew Octavian took over Octavian changed his name to Augustus and became the first Roman emperor.

The Roman army was very tough and well-trained, with experience in many wars and battles. After they conquered all of Italy, Roman solders marched into other countries and defeated their armies. The land they ruled over was called the Roman Empire.

During this period, the Romans built many fine roads, bridges, towns and cities. The towns were planned to look like Rome, with a town centre, or forum, containing magnificent government buildings and grand temples.

Eventually, the empire ran into trouble. There were riots and rebellions and attacks from tribes called barbarians. Five hundred years after Augustus's reign, the city of Rome was burnt and almost all the Empire destroyed.

Vocabulary power (page 40)

Noun	Verb	Adjective
colony	colonise	colonial
conquest	conquer	conquering
invasion	invade	invading
rebellion	rebel	rebellious
exploration	explore	exploratory
invention	invent	inventive
development	develop	developing
reign	reign	reigning

Read and learn (page 41)

Meanings (**Note:** your dictionary may have different wording.):
disintegrates = falls apart
antiquity = past ages
abundant = a large amount, plenty
casts = hollow moulds
plundered = searched to find things to steal and destroy
adorn = decorate

7 Once upon a time (pages 42–47)

Quick fun (page 42)

(in any order)
The Emperor's New Clothes
Beauty and the Beast
Little Red Riding Hood
The Muddle-Headed Wombat
The Adventures of Dot and the Kangaroo
The Adventures of Blinky Bill

Fill in the gaps (page 43)

1 ogre **2** handsome, courageous, prince **3** giant **4** castles **5** Knights, dragons, rescue **6** heroines **7** heroes **8** dungeon, tower **9** wicked, cruel, witch **10** wizards, villains

Looking at homophones (page 44)

1 **a** weather–climate; whether–if
b quite–a little; quiet–silent
c tale–story; tail–part of an animal
d lesson–study time; lesson–reduce
e aloud–with sound; allowed–permitted
f piece–bit; peace–quietness
g through–between; threw–tossed
h dye–colour; die–pass away
i strait–a narrow stretch of water; straight–direct
j weak–not strong; week–7 days
k except–but for; accept–take
l guest–visitor; guessed–predicted
m there–a place; they're–they are; their–belonging to them
n to–opposite of *from*; too–also; two–a number
o your–belonging to you; you're–you are

2 **a** They're, there, their **b** too, to, two
c accept, except **d** You're, your
e threw, through

Looking at … changing *y* to *i* (page 44)

a happier **b** easily **c** heaviness **d** carriage **e** prettier **f** carrying **g** prettiness **h** praying **i** merriment **j** spookily **k** prayer **l** hungrily **m** emptiness **n** clumsier **o** emptying

Proofreading (page 45)

My favourite fairytale is *Cinderella*. *Cinderella* has all the classic characters: the heartless, wicked stepmother, the ugly stepsisters, the handsome prince and the poor beautiful young girl. It even has a fairy godmother. When the King's son gives a ball, Cinderella is not allowed to go because of all the work she must do. However, after her silly, spiteful sisters go off, Cinderella is rescued by her godmother who waves her magic wand, converting a pumpkin to a coach, six mice into horses and six lizards into footmen. She transforms Cinderella's ragged clothes and shoes into a beautiful dress and dainty glass slippers, and then sends her off—but with a warning to return by midnight. Of course, the prince falls in love with her straight away, but when the clock chimes twelve, Cinderella dashes off into the night. Luckily, one of her slippers falls off in her haste to get away, and this enables the prince to find her the next day. To her foolish stepsisters' dismay, she and the prince marry and of course live happily ever after.

Vocabulary power (page 45)

a	magic looking glass	**b**	beautiful princess
c	wicked stepmother	**d**	enchanted forest
e	wicked witch	**f**	cruel queen
g	brave knight	**h**	ugly stepsister
i	rich merchant	**j**	faithful servant
k	poor woodcutter	**l**	magic wand
m	fire-breathing dragon	**n**	royal castle
o	gentle giant		

Dictionary search (page 45)

damsel = young woman (or maiden)
courtier = man who serves in the king's court
minstrel = musical entertainer
jester = joker, clown
charger = horse (especially one used in battle)
tailor = man who sews men's clothes
cobbler = shoemaker
moat = waterway built to completely encircle a castle

Read and learn (page 46)

1 **a** ii **b** i **c** i **d** ii **e** iii **f** iii **g** ii **h** i **i** ii **j** ii

Puzzle (page 47)

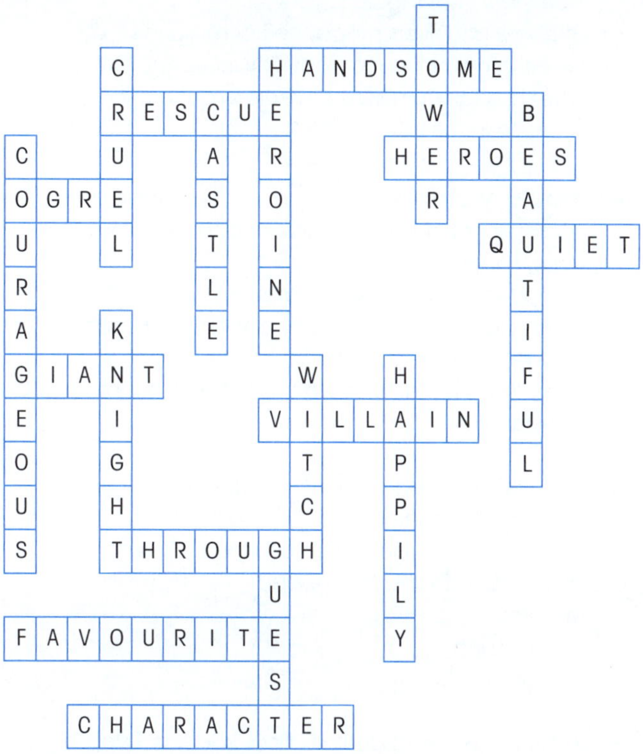

8 Water, water, everywhere (pages 48–53)

Quick fun (page 48)

1 ATLANTIC **2** ARCTIC **3** PACIFIC **4** INDIAN **5** SOUTHERN

Word scramble (page 48)

1 AQUATIC **2** FOUNTAIN **3** OCEANIC **4** LAGOON **5** HARBOUR **6** TORRENTIAL **7** BILLABONG **8** TRIBUTARY

Fill in the gaps (page 49)

1 current **2** coral, oceanic **3** marine **4** tidal **5** diluted **6** liquid **7** aquatic **8** Billabong **9** lagoon, shallow **10** fountain **11** tributary, creek **12** torrential **13** harbours

Looking at … short o sound spelt *a* (page 50)

1 **a** watt **b** twaddle **c** wadding **d** squabble **e** squalid **f** wattle **g** was **h** wallop **i** wander **j** squash **k** swap **l** waft
2 **a** wasp **b** swan **c** quarrel **d** swamp **e** swallow **f** wand

Proofreading (page 50)

Our group found out some amazing facts about water:

- Although we call our planet Earth, it is really one huge oceanic ball.
- More than 70% of the Earth's surface is covered by oceans.
- The spin of the Earth creates currents that distribute warm and cold water around the globe.
- The average depth of oceans is four kilometres.

- The Pacific covers a larger area than all the continents put together.
- Streams and rivers shape the Earth's surface by wearing away the rock they flow over. The Colorado River has taken millions of years to cut out the Grand Canyon in the USA.

Vocabulary power (pages 51–52)

1 adding small amounts of water: dampen, moisten, spray, sprinkle
adding some water: wet, water, pour
adding large amounts: slosh, drench, soak, bathe, deluge
completely covering in water: immerse, submerge, plunge, drown, flood, inundate

2 **a** wet/dampened/moistened/sprayed
b soak/submerge
c submerged/flooded/inundated
d soaked/bathed/immersed
e Pour
f drizzling
g Spray/Wet

3 **a** burble **b** slurp **c** gush **d** drip **e** squelch **f** slop **g** splash **h** squish **i** gurgle **j** plop

Read and learn (pages 52–53)

1 a **2** b **3** c **4** c **5** a **6** b **7** a

Puzzle (page 53)

a fountain **b** swamp **c** shallow **d** liquid **e** current **f** marine **g** dilute **h** Pacific **i** Southern **j** width **k** disappear **l** wan **m** squash

9 Describing people (pages 54–59)

Quick fun (page 54)

FEAT, SEAT, FAT, SAT, SAFE, SURE, ATE, EAT, SEAT, RAT, REEF, RATE, TEAR, STAR, FAR, FUR, FEAR, SEAR, TRUE, ARE, FARE, FATE, TURF, REST, FEAST

Fill in the gaps (pages 54–55)

1 scarred, extremely/rather, charming **2** ordinary, crooked **3** frizzy **4** straight, blonde, slender **5** lovely/attractive/pretty/pleasant/gorgeous **6** freckles **7** olive-skinned **8** plump **9** rather/extremely, rather/extremely **10** lovely/gorgeous **11** similar

Killer words (page 55)

weight, height, hasn't, wearing, different

Proofreading (page 55)

SUPERMARKET HOLD-UP

Police are looking for two men who held up a supermarket in Milson's Bay at around 7 p.m. last night. The older man was wearing a mask, so police are uncertain about his facial features. However, he was described by witnesses as of average height and weight with frizzy dark hair, and probably olive-skinned. He wore an unusual multi-coloured coat and extremely baggy trousers. The younger man was described as fair-skinned, with strait red hair and freckles. He was wearing old jeans and a yellow T-shirt. One witness who spoke to the man said 'The younger man had a very pleasant voice and a rather charming smile. He didn't look dangerous at all.' Police are asking the public to come forward if they have information about the two suspects.

Looking at … *ur* words (page 56)

2

a	**U**	**R**	B	A	N		
b	S	**U**	**R**	F	A	C	E
c	C	H	**U**	**R**	C	H	
d	A	B	S	**U**	**R**	D	
e	D	I	S	T	**U**	**R**	B
f		M	U	R	M	**U**	**R**
g		O	C	C	**U**	**R**	
h		S	T	**U**	**R**	D	Y
i		T	**U**	**R**	K	E	Y
j	F	**U**	**R**	T	H	E	R
k	**U**	**R**	C	H	I	N	
l	S	**U**	**R**	G	E	O	N

3 **a** surname **b** gurgles/gurgled **c** turn **d** burglar **e** curved/turned **f** purse, purchases

Looking at … comparing people and things (page 57)

sturdy, sturdier, sturdiest
pleasant, more pleasant, most pleasant
pretty, prettier, prettiest
attractive, more attractive, most attractive
frizzy, frizzier, frizziest
charming, more charming, most charming
straight, straighter, straightest
plump, plumper, plumpest
red, redder, reddest
blonde, blonder, blondest

Vocabulary power (pages 57–58)

1 **a** small and graceful **b** extremely unpleasant or ugly **c** stylish and tidily dressed (usually describing a small man) **d** healthy and attractive, able to move gracefully e graceful and attractive in appearance and behaviour f strong and simple (not delicate) g awkward and graceless in movement h graceful and thin i red (usually to describe a face) j very beautiful, delicate k having a round pretty face like a child l attracting attention because unusual or very attractive

Note: Your dictionary might use different words to explain the meanings.

2 a dainty, lithe, elegant, willowy b rugged, ruddy c hideous d dapper e willowy, exquisite, striking f ruddy, rugged g cherubic

Read and learn (pages 58–59)

1 a i b ii c i d ii e ii f i g i h ii i i j ii

2 Paragraph 2.

Puzzle (page 59)

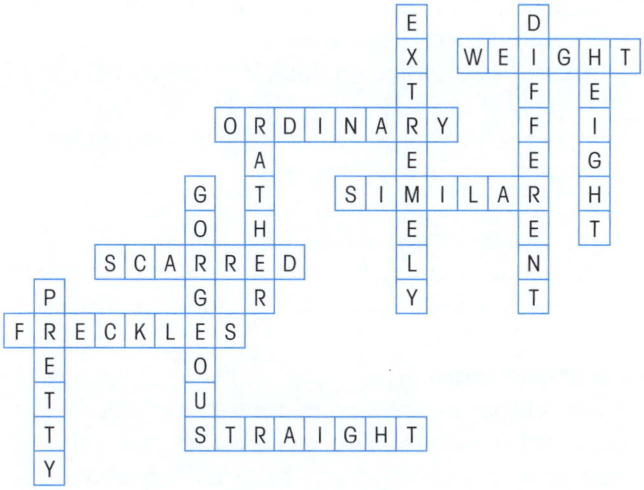

10 In the country (pages 60–65)

Quick fun (page 60)

1 MOUNTAIN 2 SWAMP 3 BILLABONG 4 DESERT 5 CREEK 6 RIVER 7 STREAM 8 LAGOON

Fill in the gaps (page 61)

1 Range 2 forest 3 paddock, field/meadow 4 scenery/landscape 5 flora, fauna 6 cliffs 7 village, national park 8 wilderness 9 environment 10 nature 11 spectacular/magnificent 12 rural 13 spacious, magnificent/spectacular

Looking at ... soft *g* and *dge* words (page 62)

1 a generous b image c germ d gigantic/huge e geology f Egypt g genius h large i lunge j gypsy

2 a GEL b GENTLE c TRAGIC d GINGER e GEOLOGY f SURGEON g IMAGINE h GYM

3 a FUDGE b JUDGE c NUDGE d SLEDGE e SMUDGE f WEDGE g HEDGE h KNOWLEDGE i PORRIDGE j TRUDGE

4 a GADGET b FIDGET c MIDGET d BUDGET

Proofreading (page 63)

We camped at the edge of a huge forest. The scenery was absolutely spectacular, but we were far too nervous to care much about it. The cliffs we had earlier thought magnificent, we now saw as threatening. Although we had really wanted to experience nature, somehow it did not seem so important now that we were lost and alone. We would probably not go much further than the paddocks at the end of our town from now on. The only fauna we wanted to see were our pet cats and dogs. We knew there was a small village about ten miles away and we decided we would aim for that the next day. We tried to settle down to sleep, but before too long the quiet was broken by a disturbing rustle.

Vocabulary power (page 63)

1 a cliffs: towering, steep, rocky
b fields: green, open, grassy
c forest: deep, dark, dense
d village: pretty, picturesque, quaint
e landscape: bleak, dramatic, rugged
f wilderness: barren, desolate, unspoilt
g river: mighty, winding, swollen

2 breathtaking, dramatic, spectacular, stunning, superb, delightful, glorious, wonderful

Read and learn (page 64)

1 c 2 a 3 c 4 b 5 a 6 a

Puzzle (pages 64–65)

1 a FI**E**LD b RA**N**GE
c **V**ILLAGE d CL**I**FF
e RU**R**AL f FL**O**RA
g FAU**N**A h **M**EADOW
i SC**E**NERY j **N**ATURAL
k MAGNIFICEN**T**
ENVIRONMENT

2 a **P**I**C**TURE b INSTEA**D**
c GEOGR**A**PHY d DA**N**GEROU**S**
e GYMN**A**STICS f A**L**THOUGH
g QUI**E**T
LANDSCAPE

Review 2 (pages 66–69)

Which word? (page 69)

1 except 2 allowed 3 piece 4 through 5 quite 6 they're 7 your

11 Moving around (pages 70–75)

Quick fun (page 70)

COME	SWIMS
CORE	SLIMS
CARE	SLAMS
BARE	CLAMS
BARK	CLAWS
BACK	CRAWS
	CRAWL

Word scramble (page 70)

1 MOTION **2** WANDERED **3** HURRYING **4** RAPIDLY **5** GRADUALLY **6** BACKWARDS **7** FOLLOWED **8** SUDDENLY

Fill in the gaps (page 71)

1 accelerated **2** backwards, forwards, movement **3** gradually **4** wriggled/squirmed **5** mobile **6** wandering **7** hurrying **8** crawled **9** velocity **10** motionless, swiftly **11** haste **12** rapidly

Looking at … *ir* words (page 72)

birth, circular, fir, firm, firstly, flirt, girder, mirth, quirky, shirt, sir, skirmish, skirt, squirm, squirt, stir, swirl, third, thirsty, thirty, twirl, virgin, virtue, whirl

The spelling ***ir*** occurs more often after these consonant sounds: ***f***, ***th***.

Looking at … doubling (pages 72–73)

1 **a** tripped, tripping **b** digger, digging **c** beginner, beginning **d** quarrelled, quarrelling **e** tunnelled, tunnelling **f** jogged, jogging

2 **a** no **b** no **c** no **d** yes **e** no **f** yes **g** yes **h** yes

Proofreading (page 73)

I was in the car with my Mum and Dad on the way to the most important rhythmic gymnastics competition of the year. I had nearly won last year and was determined that this time I would definitely come first. The traffic had been terrible all the way and I was getting very worried. Now it was completely stationary. I rocked backwards and forwards on my seat, and fiddled with my uniform. Then I started practising my gym movements. Dad told me to stop squirming around. Suddenly, we accelerated. The traffic gradually began to clear. I asked Mum if I could ring Mariella on the mobile and see where she was. 'No', she and Dad shouted with one voice. 'Just sit still. We'll be there in thirty seconds.' Well, we did get there in time. And I did win. Dad reckoned it was because I got so much time to practise in the back seat!

Vocabulary power (page 73)

1 saunter = walk in a slow and relaxed way, often in no particular direction
plod = walk slowly as if your feet are heavy
trudge = walk slowly with a lot of effort
lumber = move slowly and awkwardly
swoop = move very quickly but smoothly from a height (as a bird) or make a sudden attack
scamper = run with small, quick steps
slither = move smoothly over a surface
slouch = walk, sit or stand with shoulders and head bent slightly over
scurry = move quickly with small, quick steps (like scamper)
stride = walk quickly with long steps
shuffle = walk pulling your feet along the ground, not lifting them
amble = walk in a slow and relaxed way
prance = walk in an energetic way, with more movement than necessary
toddle = walk with short steps, trying to keep the body balanced
dawdle = walk or do something very slowly, taking more time than is necessary

2 **a** dawdle, slouch, shuffle **b** swoop
c trudge, plod, slouch, lumber **d** lumber, amble, plod
e lumber, shuffle, dawdle **f** scamper, scurry

Read and learn (page 74)

You should have underlined at least some of these:
paragraph 1: wander, glide, dip, lunge, lift, tilt
paragraph 2: jumping up and down, cruised sedately, turned, dancing about
paragraph 3: hurled, lurch, drifted quietly
paragraph 5: wandered, stomped, rushed
paragraph 6: crawled low, zigzagging commando style, preening, reached, sprang from his starting blocks, began its take off, waddle, run, with wings outstretched and pumping, took three paces, started to lift off, dived full-length, rugby tackled, thrashed about, churned with panic, squeezed, flapping wings, delivered left and right hooks and the odd jab and uppercut

Puzzle (page 75)

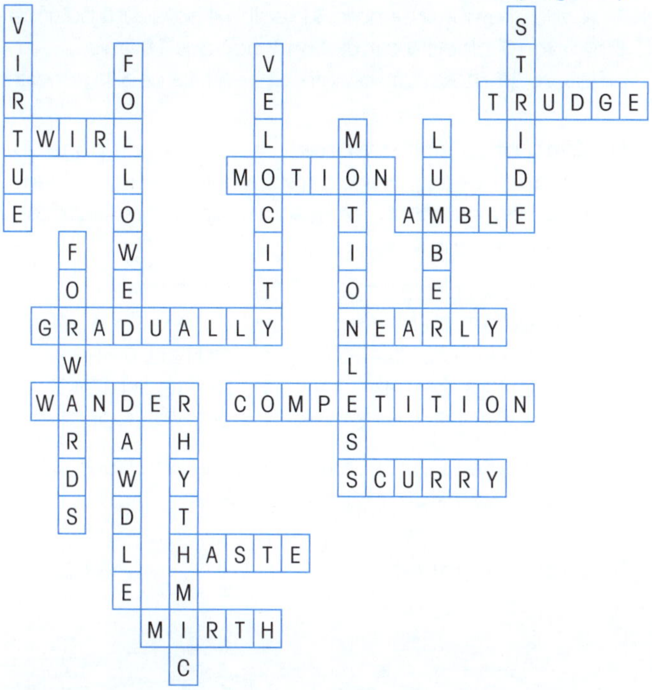

12 Working with mathematics (pages 76–81)

Quick fun (page 76)

1 NINETY. If you take TY away from it, you have NINE left
2 If you write the numbers as Roman numerals: take I (1) away from XIX (19) and get XX (20).
3 SHORT. If you add ER to it, it becomes SHORTER!

Fill in the gaps (page 77)

1 graph **2** quarter **3** digit **4** estimated **5** percentage **6** fraction, decimal **7** multiplied, divided **8** multiplication, subtraction **9** addition, division **10** amount **11** minus, equals **12** average **13** total **14** decrease

Killer words (page 77)

enough, answer, exactly, either, neither

Looking at ... *sion* words (pages 78–79)

1 ***sh*** sound: tension, extension, suspension, dimension, comprehension
zh sound: excursion, confusion, conclusion, decision, erosion, explosion, vision, division, television, revision, occasion, persuasion, version
2 **a** excursion **b** vision **c** tension **d** division **e** conclusion **f** comprehension **g** confusion **h** dimension
3 **a** television, division, revision
b i tend **ii** extend **iii** suspend **iv** comprehend **v** decide **vi** erode **vii** explode **viii** persuade

Word scramble (page 79)

1 ADDITION **2** SUBTRACTION **3** ESTIMATE **4** PERCENTAGE **5** FRACTION **6** MULTIPLICATION **7** DECIMAL **8** DIVISION

Proofreading (page 79)

average	graph	answer
plus	multiplied	enough
addition	percentage	either
divide	amount	division
minus	quarter	extension
decrease	equal	total

Vocabulary power (page 80)

1 **a** able to speak many languages
b a large crowd
c act on each other
d destroy itself
e take out, something taken out (e.g. of a book)

2 **a** multicultural **b** suburb **c** supervise **d** automobile **e** predict **f** interrupt **g** external **h** transform

Read and learn (page 81)

1 b **2** a **3** b **4** a **5** c **6** a

Puzzle (page 81)

TOTAL, DIGIT, MINUS, PLUS

13 Experimenting and building (pages 82–87)

Quick fun (page 82)

BLUE, RED, YELLOW, PINK, BROWN, BLACK, ORANGE, VIOLET, GREEN, PURPLE, WHITE

Fill in the gaps (page 83)

1 timber, metal **2** rubbish **3** design **4** material **5** equipment/material **6** procedure/instructions **7** piece, cardboard **8** method, scissors **9** build **10** carefully/gently **11** Collect **12** gently/carefully **13** separate **14** science, experiments **15** instructions

Looking at ... long e sound spelt *ie* (page 84)

1 **a** tier **b** field **c** shriek **d** brief **e** grief **f** pier **g** piece **h** priest **i** siege **j** thief **k** chief **l** relieve **m** achieve **n** relief
2 **a** shield **b** pierce **c** shriek **d** grief **e** relief **f** pieces **g** chief **h** thief **i** achieve **j** believe **k** fierce **l** priest

Looking at ... *ic* and *al* adjectives (page 84)

1 graphic **2** acidic **3** basic **4** cubic **5** rhythmic(al) **6** periodic **7** strategic **8** dynamic **9** volcanic **10** historic(al) **11** magnetic **12** essential **13** digital **14** substantial **15** accidental **16** ideal **17** practical **18** metric(al)

Proofreading (page 85)

During the year, we had Science Club meetings once a fortnight on Wednesday afternoons. We did lots of interesting experiments, although sometimes we didn't follow Mr Tran's instructions carefully enough, and things did not turn out quite right. We used lots of scientific equipment like microscopes, test tubes and beakers. However, mostly we used recycled rubbish from home and everyday materials that we had in the classroom. Jackson's father supplied us with timber and metal from his work, and the local supermarket let us have as many cardboard boxes as we wanted. My favourite day was when we constructed bridges using only newspaper and sticky tape and scissors. The funniest day was when Jackie let out all the ants from the ant farm and they got into the staffroom.

Vocabulary power (pages 85–86)

1 know or understand something very well: know something backwards; know something inside out; know something like the back of your hand
not know or understand something at all: be in over your head; be in the dark; be out of your depth
eventually understand something: see the light; get the picture; get the hang of something
put in a lot of effort: work your guts out; work your fingers to the bone; move mountains

2 a worked his guts out/worked his fingers to the bone/moved mountains
b saw the light/got the picture/got the hang of it
c out of my depth/in over my head (*in the dark* is not as good here)
d knows … backwards/knows … inside out/knows … like the back of his hand

Read and learn (page 86)

2 a i **b** ii **c** ii **d** i **e** ii

Puzzle (page 87)

1 **a** build **b** scissors **c** science **d** drawing

2 **a** **pie**ce (pie) **b** **mat**erial (mat) **c** **gent**ly (gent) **d** dia**gram** (gram) **e** **met**hod (met) **f** pat**tern** (tern) **g** colou**red** (red) **h** card**boa**rd (boa) **i** **car**efully/**car**dboard (car) **j** d**raw**ing (raw) **k** sepa**rate** (rate)

14 A healthy body (pages 88–93)

Quick fun (page 88)

HEAL, HEAT, HATE, HALE, THY, BOY, TOY, LATE, LATHE, LOB, DOB, HOB, BYE, BY, DYE, HE, THE, BYTE (a computer term), BOTH, BEAT, DATE, BADE, HEAD, BED, BEAD, DEBT, BET, LEA (a meadow), HALT, TALE (You might have found others.)

Fill in the gaps (page 89)

1 muscles, human **2** Genetic **3** breathe **4** physical **5** balance **6** skeleton **7** blood **8** circulation **9** nervous **10** cells, emotions **11** muscular strength **12** heart **13** healthy, energy

Looking at … soft c words (page 90)

1 advance, ceiling, cellar, census, central, certain, citizen, citrus, city, civilization, excellent, except, fancy, fascinate, notice, recent, recite, sentence, service, twice

2 **a** RECENT, CERTAIN **b** FANCY, CITY
c EXCEPT, CENTRAL **d** CITIZEN, EXCELLENT
e TWICE, FASCINATE **f** CENSUS, CEILING
g CITRUS, CELLAR **h** RECITE, SENTENCE
i ADVANCE, CIVILISATION **j** SERVICE, NOTICE

3 ac**c**elerate (unit 11), per**c**entage, de**c**imal (unit 12) pro**c**edure, pie**c**e, **sc**issors (unit 13)

Vocabulary power (page 91)

1

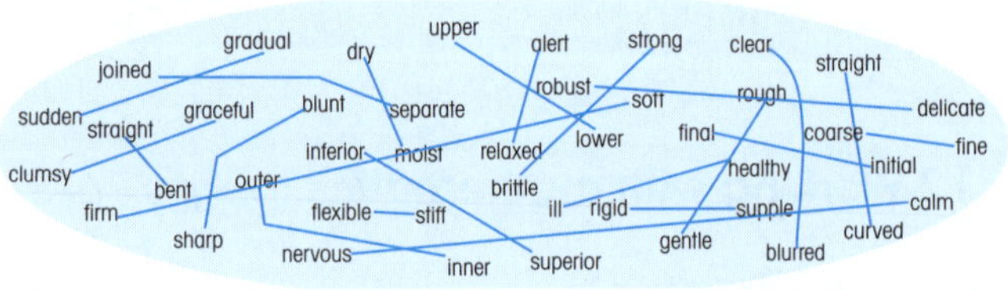

2 **a** colourless **b** unsteady **c** immobile **d** insensitive **e** incomplete **f** independent **g** inflexible **h** infrequent **i** impractical **j** fearless **k** useless **l** immature **m** impure **n** inactive **o** inattentive **p** extraordinary

Proofreading (page 91)

human	circulation	laughter
exercise	skeleton	stomach
genes	cells	twice
muscle	breath	certain
heart	physical	except
blood	energy	service
nervous	strength	sentence
activity	body	living

Read and learn (page 92)

1 reaction **2** belong **3** vomit **4** out **5** expel **6** useful **7** tightens **8** hopelessness

Puzzle (page 93)

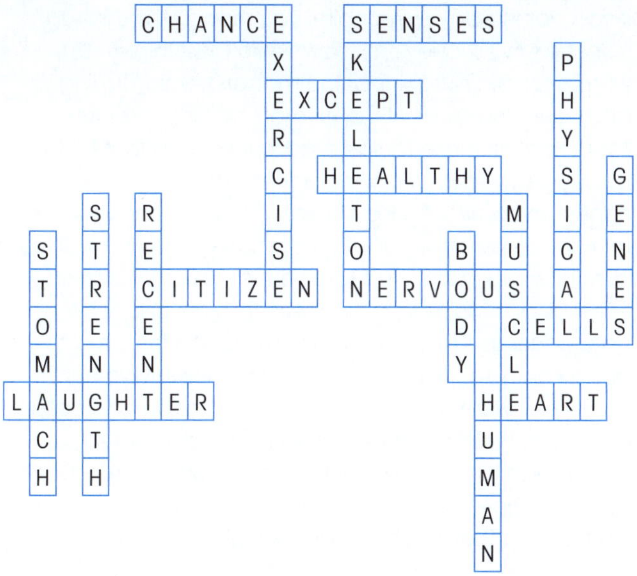

15 Talking about time (pages 94–99)

Quick fun (page 94)

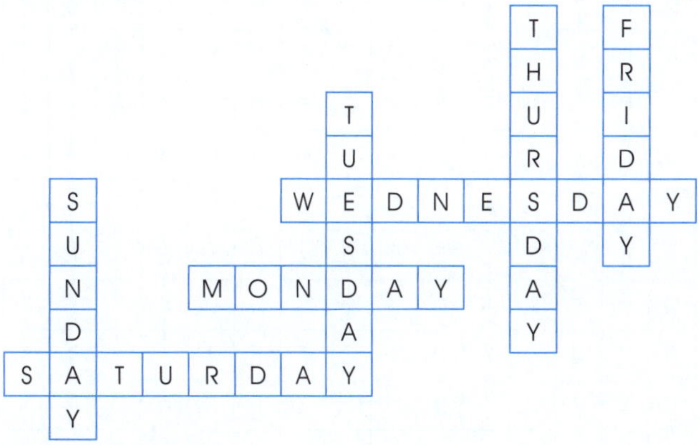

Fill in the gaps (page 95)

1 future **2** millennium **3** moment, afterwards **4** fortnight, monthly **5** yesterday, tomorrow **6** beforehand **7** schedule **8** decade **9** immediately **10** twenties **11** past **12** nowadays, thousand

Looking at … ordinal numbers (page 96)

1

first	seventh	thirteenth	nineteenth
second	eighth	fourteenth	twentieth
third	ninth	fifteenth	thirtieth
fourth	tenth	sixteenth	ninetieth
fifth	eleventh	seventeenth	hundredth
sixth	twelfth	eighteenth	thousandth

2 **a** TWELFTH **b** TWENTIETH **c** THIRD **d** THIRTEENTH **e** THOUSANDTH **f** FIRST **g** FIFTH **h** EIGHTH **i** FORTIETH **j** FOURTH

Looking at … contractions (pages 96–97)

1 **a** She'll be turning one hundred next month. We're giving her a big party.
b The children aren't going to the celebration tomorrow. They're very disappointed.
c We won't have our weekly test today. I've changed it to next Monday.
d If you studied harder, you'd pass easily. I'm sure you know that.
e We've told you a thousand times already, but you just haven't listened.
f Who's registered for tomorrow's program? Isn't everyone going?
g He didn't know she'd moved to the city.
h Don't tell anyone you're coming. It'll be a surprise.

2 **a** its **b** it's **c** Its **d** It's **e** It's **f** It's **g** its **h** It's

Proofreading (page 97)

My great-grandparents grew up in the first few decades of the 20th century. They're both in their nineties now, but they still tell me stories about what it was like all those years ago. Yesterday, when I went to see them, they told me about what they used to do for entertainment at night when they were young. They said that they'd spend hours after dinner reading books or listening to music on the gramophone—a kind of record player. Sometimes they even used to dance at home. On the weekends, they often went out to visit friends and occasionally they went to dances at the town hall. Afterwards, they would walk around the town and meet up with other friends for an ice-cream or a cup of tea. Nowadays, they still like to listen to music, but they usually watch television like us. They're always saying that it was better in the old days.

Vocabulary power (page 98)

1 **a** shortly **b** moment
c continuous **d** frequently
e short **f** promptly
g temporary **h** eternal
i final **j** eventually
k previously **l** subsequently
m currently **n** simultaneously

2 **a** continuous **b** simultaneously **c** currently **d** frequently **e** temporary **f** eternal **g** promptly **h** shortly

Puzzle (page 98)

Three words: past, present, future.

What am I? The letter ***m***.

Read and learn (page 99)

1 **a** shutter telegraph **b** morse code telegraph **c** radio transmission **d** semaphore

2 **a** F **b** T **c** T **d** T

3 A mobile phone base station is compared to a semaphore station.

Review 3 (pages 100–103)

Which word? (page 103)

1 it's **2** who's **3** hour **4** past **5** You're **6** They're

16 Money, money, money (pages 104–109)

Quick fun (page 104)

1 MILLION, MILL, ILL, LION, LAIR, AIR, MARE, LIE, RAIL, MAIN, RAIN, RAM, RIM, LILO, IRON, RAN, MAN, MEN, NOR, NIL, AIL, RE, LOIN, ON, AN, ROLL, MELON, LEMON, LIME, LAME, MALE, LINE, ROAM, REMAIN (You might have found others.)

2 **a** PLAZA **b** MALL **c** ARCADE **d** CENTRE **e** MARKET **f** SQUARE

Word scramble (page 104)

1 UNIQUE **2** CATALOGUE **3** PURCHASES **4** EXPENSIVE **5** ESSENTIALS **6** BARGAIN **7** SUITABLE **8** ADVERTISEMENT

Fill in the gaps (page 105)

1 budget, essentials **2** appliances, aisles **3** millionaire **4** receipts, exchange, suitable **5** purchases, persuade, bargains **6** catalogues, department **7** advertisement, discounts **8** quality, unique **9** quantities **10** extravagant

Looking at ... *en*, *an*, *ain*, *in*, *ine*, *on* and *ern* words (page 106)

1 **a** crimson **b** modern **c** bargain **d** slogan **e** token **f** rotten **g** captain **h** villain **i** eastern/western/southern/northern **j** govern **k** demon **l** bulletin **m** masculine

2 **a** LANTERN **b** POLLEN **c** TALON **d** TURBAN **e** GREMLIN **f** DETERMINE **g** PATTERN **h** JAVELIN

Vocabulary power (pages 107–108)

1 **a** PEDESTRIAN **b** CONTRADICT **c** DEPEND **d** REJECT **e** INTERRUPT **f** TERMINATE

2 **a** one who tells his subjects exactly what to do **b** something which hangs around your neck **c** throw or force out **d** does not work anymore (broken) or does not do the right thing anymore (bad person) **e** because the trip ends there **f** feet

4 **a** iii **b** ii **c** ii **d** i **e** i **f** ii

Read and learn (page 108)

1 tight with money—not letting go of it from his hands

2 squeezing, wrenching, grasping, scraping, clutching

3 wanting everything, especially what other people have got

4 c

5 b

6 'Scrooge' is an insulting term because many people know the Charles Dickens character and how he was only interested in money and his own selfish needs. Sometimes, however, you might hear people use the term in a joking way, e.g. *You old Scrooge!*

Proofreading (page 109)

If you want to be a millionaire, you should start thinking about saving money right now. Try to resist those wonderful little bargains at the markets. Avoid strolling up and down the aisles of department stores just for fun. Learn to resist those fantastic advertisements that try to persuade you that a particular piece of clothing is necessary to avoid a life of misery! Most people who end up rich are very careful with their money. They think about every cent they spend, examine every receipt and check every bit of change they are given. They never look through catalogues just to fill time—they might be tempted to buy something! Most of them began their saving habits when they were small children—putting aside one dollar when they were given two, asking their parents if they could keep the five cent pieces they didn't want. So don't think that these people are unique in any way. They are just like you. They just take care of their money.

Puzzle (page 109)

D	P	Q	D	I	S	C	O	U	N	T	D	Y	V	E
E	U	U	B	O	U	G	H	T	N	D	D	T	S	S
R	R	A	P	E	R	S	U	A	D	E	H	Q	U	S
A	C	L	A	Z	S	O	G	T	Y	H	G	U	I	E
Y	H	I	N	E	Y	A	R	B	U	Y	B	A	T	N
U	A	T	Q	I	V	P	H	M	A	B	A	N	A	T
N	S	Y	P	A	I	D	B	C	B	R	R	T	B	I
I	E	A	R	U	E	Z	U	Z	R	W	G	I	L	A
Q	S	T	P	K	O	U	D	S	D	U	A	T	E	L
U	X	Q	V	A	R	T	G	A	F	A	I	Y	I	S
E	X	C	H	A	N	G	E	Z	L	R	N	O	G	N
S	R	A	D	V	E	R	T	I	S	E	M	E	N	T
Z	M	O	N	E	Y	L	R	E	C	E	I	P	T	A
A	I	S	L	E	T	N	E	C	E	S	S	A	R	Y

17 Saving our planet (pages 110–115)

Quick fun (page 110)

a Earth 3 **b** Mercury 1 **c** Venus 2 **d** Jupiter 5 **e** Mars 4 **f** Neptune 8 **g** Saturn 6 **h** Uranus 7

Pluto is the one no longer considered a planet.

Fill in the gaps (page 111)

1 plastic **2** awareness, community, environment **3** recycled **4** waste, behaviour **5** pollution **6** garbage/waste **7** chemicals, toxic **8** reduce **9** compost **10** destroyed **11** protection **12** ozone layer **13** Climate **14** resources, responsibility, conserve

Killer words (page 111)

neighbours, amongst, whole, hole, choice

Looking at … irregular verbs (page 112)

1 **a** caught **b** ridden **c** shown **d** worn **e** blown **f** heard/knew/left **g** shook **h** bought **i** drove/rode **j** drew

2 pay, paid, paid; tear, tore, torn; wake, woke, woken; think, thought, thought; teach, taught, taught; write, wrote, written; sing, sang, sung; sleep, slept, slept

Vocabulary power (page 113)

1 **a** *anti* = against **b** *bio* = life **c** *graph* = write **d** *mono* = one **e** *micro* = small **f** *syn* = with, together, **g** *therm* = heat **h** *metre/meter* = measure

2 **a** anticlimax = something disappointing because it was expected to be exciting (e.g. a story ending which lets you down)

b micrometer = a device used for measuring very small things and making exact measurements

c monochrome = one colour

d monopoly = having power or control especially in business (think of the boardgame *Monopoly*)

e monotonous = not changing (the one tone), so boring

f synagogue = where Jewish people come together to worship

Proofreading (page 113)

garbage	destroyed	shown
chemical	waste	meant
plastic	environment	caught
toxic	climate	worn
resources	compost	pollution
conserve	community	choice
protection	reduce	amongst
ozone layer	recycling	neighbour

Read and learn (page 114)

1 **a** ii **b** ii **c** i **d** ii **e** i **f** ii **g** ii **h** ii

2 b

3 autopsy

Word scramble (page 115)

1 GARBAGE **2** REDUCE **3** CHEMICAL **4** ENVIRONMENT **5** PROTECTION **6** DESTROY **7** RECYCLE **8** PLASTIC

Puzzle (page 115)

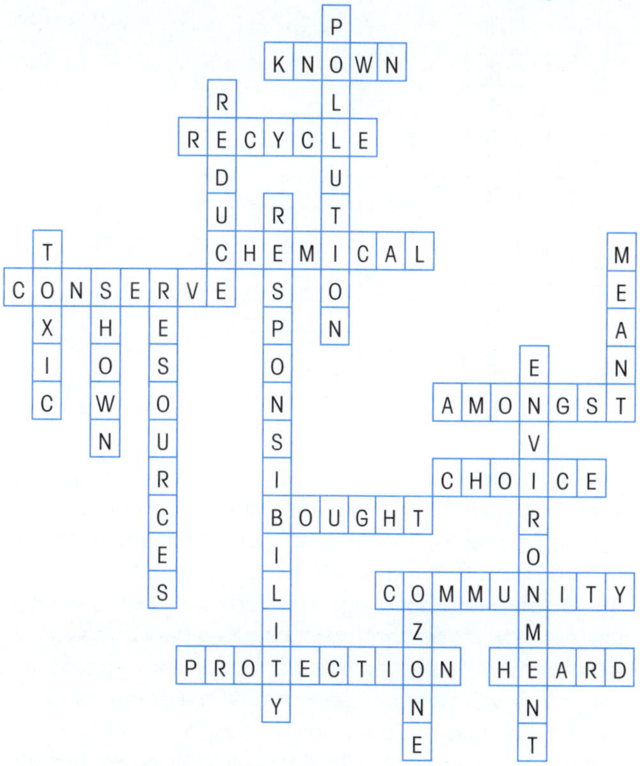

18 Different cultures (pages 116–121)

Quick fun (page 116)

1 ENG**L**ISH
2 IR**A**QI
3 INDO**N**ESIAN
4 **G**ERMAN
5 PORT**U**GUESE
6 RUSSI**A**N
7 E**G**YPTIAN
8 GRE**E**K
9 CHINE**S**E

LANGUAGES

Fill in the gaps (page 117)

1 traditional **2** differences **3** society **4** behaviour **5** familiar, prejudice **6** fascinating, customs/beliefs/attitudes **7** foreign, cultures/societies **8** gestures, language **9** social **10** customs/attitudes/beliefs—both answers **11** attitude **12** acceptance, respect

Looking at … words with the prefixes ex- and exc-
(page 118)

a	**E**	**X**	I	T					
b	**E**	**X**	I	L	E				
c	**E**	**X**	O	T	I	C			
d	**E**	**X**	H	I	B	I	T		
e	**E**	**X**	E	R	C	I	S	E	
f	**E**	**X**	H	A	U	S	T	E	D
g	**E**	**X**	C	E	P	T	I	O	N
h	**E**	**X**	C	E	L	L	E	N	T
i	**E**	**X**	A	M	P	L	E		
j	**E**	**X**	C	E	E	D			
k	**E**	**X**	P	E	L				
l	**E**	**X**	A	M					

Proofreading
(page 119)

When you travel to a foreign land, it is a good idea to become familiar with the face, hand and body gestures used by people in that region to communicate meaning. This is called body language. For example, English-speaking cultures show agreement by nodding their heads. They show disagreement by shaking their heads from side to side. It can be very surprising to see that there are differences in the way other people use body language. In some cultures, for example, the English gesture for *no* means *yes*.

Body language also includes how much we touch each other and how close we stand to each other. There are sometimes gender or age differences, but usually there are unwritten rules in every society about these matters. South Americans, for example, touch each other during conversations much more than the French. The British hardly touch at all. This behaviour can cause serious communication problems.

Vocabulary power
(page 119)

eat your words—accept your opinion was wrong; get hold of the wrong end of the stick—misunderstand what someone is saying; get your wires crossed—misunderstand each other; be on the same wavelength—understand each other well; speak with forked tongue—tell lies; say it in words of one syllable—say something very clearly; can't get a word in edgeways—not be able to be heard because people are talking too much; be stuck/lost for words—not be able to think of anything to say; have a word in your ear—say something secretly so that others don't hear; put words in your mouth—tell you what you should say and think; take words out of your mouth—someone says exactly what you wanted to say

Read and learn
(page 120)

1 b **2** a **3** b **4** a **5** a **6** b **7** b **8** a **9** b **10** a

Puzzle
(page 121)

1 culture **2** foreign **3** gesture **4** respect **5** familiar **6** language **7** customs **8** belief **9** modern **10** acceptance **11** prejudice **12** behaviour

19 The world of art
(pages 122–127)

Quick fun
(page 122)

1 PICASSO **2** MICHELANGELO **3** LEONARDO DA VINCI **4** REMBRANDT **5** VAN GOGH

Fill in the gaps
(page 123)

1 created, masterpiece **2** sketch **3** portrait, cartoons **4** perspective **5** realistic, colourful **6** abstract, skilful **7** artistic, drawing/sculpture **8** illustrations **9** Sculpture **10** exhibition, gallery, mural

Looking at … *ure* words
(page 124)

1 agriculture, azure, caricature, culture, departure, enclosure, fracture, furniture, injure, leisure, measure, pasture, picture, pressure, puncture, seizure, signature, texture, torture, treasure

2 ***t***, ***s***, ***z***

Proofreading
(page 124)

Our class went into the city last week to visit the Art Gallery. I wasn't sure what to expect. I knew I would see lots of paintings and sculptures, and we did see lots of these. I liked the abstract paintings best because of the brilliant colours and designs, but most of the class preferred the realistic ones—pictures of landscapes and portraits of famous people. However, I was surprised to see furniture, cloth, metal and other strange materials all twisted and moulded into funny forms. Our teacher explained that this was all modern art, and that artists used many materials and techniques these days to create their masterpieces. We also saw some very colourful graffiti in a special exhibition. These pieces were absolutely huge, covering whole walls sometimes. Some of the graffiti included illustrations and cartoons as well. They showed that graffiti art takes skill and artistic ability just like other kinds of art. I think we all appreciate art a lot more now after our excursion.

Vocabulary power
(page 125)

1 *fete* (French)–a festival or a form of entertainment, usually outdoors; *prima donna* (Italian)–a person who gets emotional and causes difficulty; *rendezvous* (French)–a meeting; *entree* (French)–the first course in a meal; *entrepreneur* (French)–a person who organises risky projects, especially in the entertainment business; *resume* (French)–a summary, usually of work experience; *ad lib* (Latin)–speak or act without a script, improvise; *et cetera* (Latin)–and so on; *taboo* (Tongan)–something forbidden in a culture; *carafe* (Italian)–jug;

siesta (Spanish)–an afternoon nap; *karaoke* (Japanese)–singing along to recorded music; *wok* (Chinese)–a deep, circular cooking pan

2 siesta, fete, café, prima donna, carafes, wok, entrepreneur

Read and learn (page 126)

1 a **2** b **3** a **4** b **5** b **6** b **7** a **8** a **9** a **10** b **11** a **12** b

Puzzle (page 127)

1 **a** **car**toon (car) **b** s**kill** (kill) **c** por**trait** (trait) **d** **master**piece (master) **e** cre**ate** (ate) **f** illust**rat**ion (rat) **g** g**all**ery (all) **h** graf**fit**i (fit) **i** exhi**bit**ion (bit) **j** col**our**ful (our) **k** sur**prise** (rise) **l** dra**wing** (wing)

2
a MURA**L**
b **A**RTISTIC
c TECH**N**IQUE
d AU**D**IENCE
e **S**KILFUL
f **C**OLOURFUL
g **A**BSTRACT
h **P**ERSPECTIVE
i SURPRIS**E**
LANDSCAPE

20 Wind, fire and rain (pages 128–133)

Quick fun (page 128)

CAT, CAST, CART, CAP, TASTE, PASTE, HASTE, ROPE, SOAP, COAT, HAT, HOPE, STAR, STEP, STOP, SHOP, POT, POST, POACH, HOP, TOP, SORT, TEA, SEA, TEAR, NEAR, STORE, CORE, HEAT, ACT, PACT, TRAP (You might have found others.)

Fill in the gaps (page 129)

1 conditions **2** weather **3** extreme, blizzards **4** calm, freakish **5** tsunami, injuries **6** drought **7** hurricanes, tornadoes, cyclones **8** tropical, catastrophe **9** bushfires, lightning, thunderstorms

Looking at … silent consonants (page 130)

1

foreign	climb	subtle	doubt	gnash
gnome	honour	gnarled	gnaw	folk
knowledge	salmon	honest	solemn	moisten
damn	design	resign	heir	condemn
psychology	knuckle	column	knot	wrestle
wreak	receipt	psychic	fasten	wreck

silent g: foreign, gnome, design, gnarled, resign, gnaw, gnash
silent k: knowledge, knuckle, knot
silent n: damn, column, solemn, condemn
silent p: psychology, receipt, psychic
silent w: wreak, wrestle, wreck
silent b: climb, subtle, doubt
silent h: honour, honest, heir
silent l: salmon, folk
silent t: fasten, moisten

2 **a** resign **b** gnome **c** wrestle **d** wreck **e** foreign **f** folk **g** knuckle **h** subtle **i** gnarled **j** gnaw

3 **a** gnash **b** heir **c** wreak **d** gnome **e** subtle **f** wrestle **g** knot **h** condemn **i** solemn **j** honour

Proofreading (page 130)

thunderstorm	blizzard	cyclone
calm	accident	blowing
bushfire	doubt	freakish
lightning	honour	catastrophe
hurricane	tornado	extreme
scared	damage	wreck
flood	torrential	column
drought	tsunami	receipt

Vocabulary power (page 131)

1 fire: raging, fierce
rain: heavy, driving, lashing, pouring, steady, torrential
wind: fierce, gale-force, stiff, strong, blustery, howling
storm: ferocious, fierce, raging, violent, freak
sunshine: blazing, brilliant, dazzling

2 Very good weather: fine, glorious, superb, lovely, great, fair, stupendous, brilliant
Ordinary weather: overcast, reasonable, gloomy
Very bad weather: dismal, atrocious, miserable, foul, nasty, dreadful, terrible, lousy, appalling, grim, vile

Read and learn (page 132)

1 scudding, swirling water; stormy sea; drowned valley; sleet; river … hissing past

2 battering wind; howling gust of wind; tore Barney from its trunk; wind pressing hard against his back; wind punched him in the side

3 staggered against the wind; began to totter down the hill; watched his feet shuffle a long way ahead of his body; he became a walking, running sail; hunched against the sleet; plodded along the road; he stepped sideways to recover his balance

4 grey, turbulent and frightened

Puzzle (page 133)

Solution on next page.

Review 4 (pages 134–137)

Which word? (page 137)

1 accept **2** except **3** aloud **4** allowed **5** hole **6** whole

Puzzle

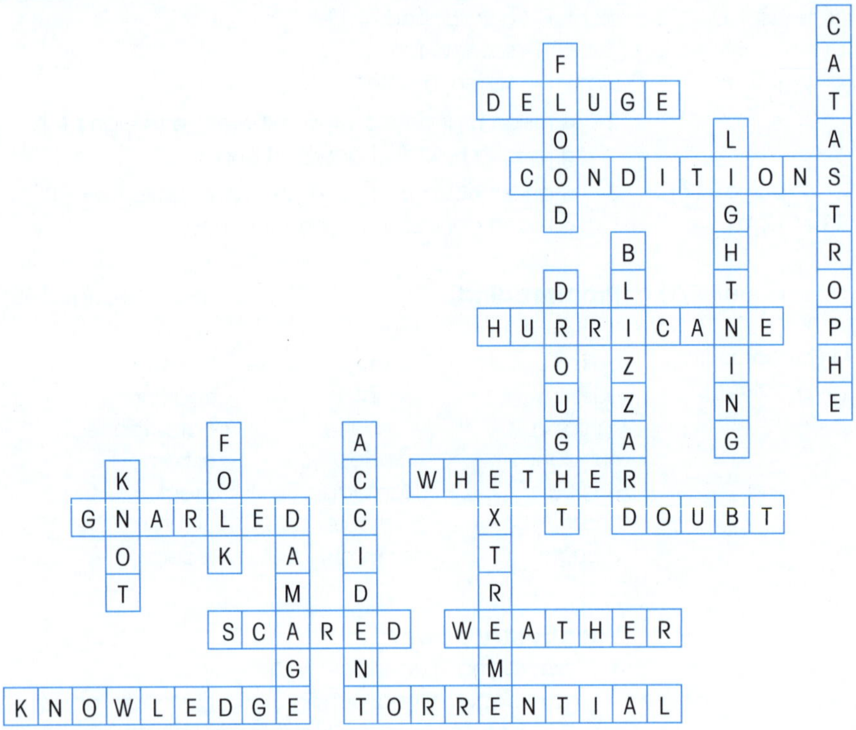
DELUGE
FLOOD
CATASTROPHE
CONDITIONS
LIGHTNING
BLIZZARD
DROUGHT
HURRICANE
FOLK
ACCIDENT
KNOT
WHETHER
GNARLED
DAMAGE
EXTREME
DOUBT
SCARED
WEATHER
KNOWLEDGE
TORRENTIAL